London A to Z

Robert S. Kane's A to Z World Travel Guides

LONDON A TO Z

PARIS A TO Z

GRAND TOUR A TO Z: THE CAPITALS OF EUROPE

EASTERN EUROPE A TO Z

SOUTH PACIFIC A TO Z

CANADA A TO Z

ASIA A TO Z

SOUTH AMERICA A TO Z

AFRICA A TO Z

Robert S. Kane

LONDON
A to Z

DOUBLEDAY & COMPANY, INC.

GARDEN CITY, NEW YORK

For Florence Fletcher

Research Editor: Max Drechsler
Map of London: Rafael Palacios

ISBN: 0-385-08637-7 Trade
0-385-08649-0 Paperback
Library of Congress Catalog Card Number 73–9035
Copyright © 1974 by Robert S. Kane
All Rights Reserved
Printed in the United States of America

Contents

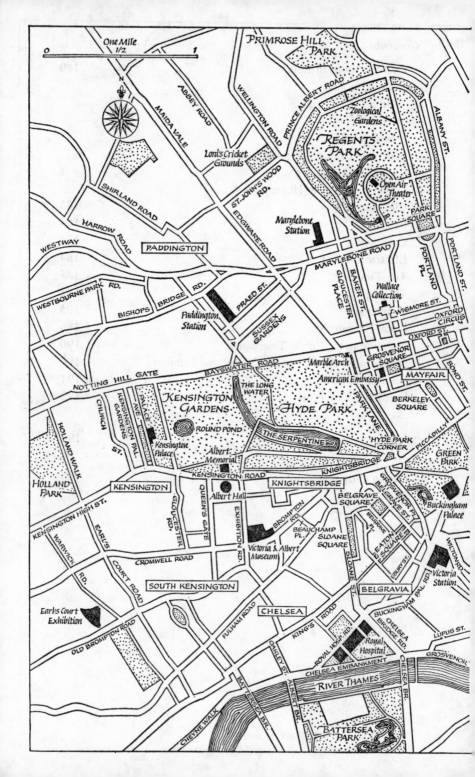

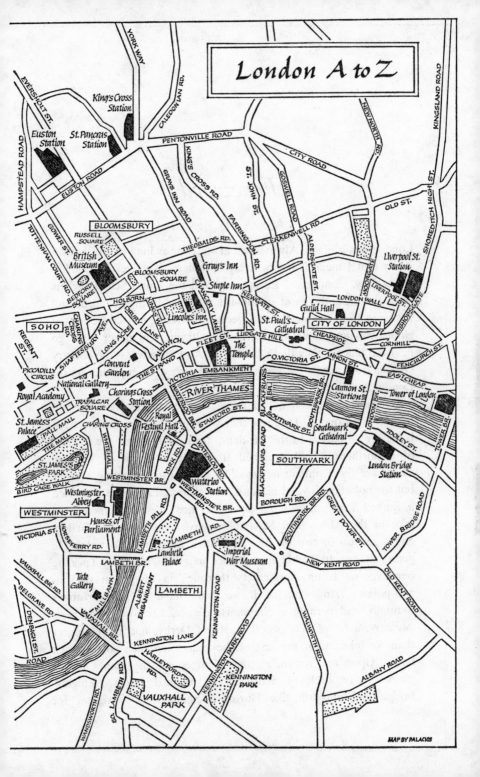

Foreword

London has it made. Always has, at least for as long as I've known it. By that I mean it has no image problem. It's Everybody's Favorite City. Continental Europeans from the south, Scandinavians from the east, the most nationalist of Scots from the north and Irishmen from the west, former colonials from every corner of the globe who are now Commonwealth citizens and never need go near the place if they don't choose to. And ourselves—the country cousins from across the water. We have always been pushovers for London.

Which is not at all a bad thing. Neither for us, nor for that matter, for London. It is just that we are not always sure why it is we are so partial to this oft-damp town tucked into the interior of a northern island detached from the continent of Europe. There are those among us who like it not for the wrong reasons but for not enough valid reasons. The visitor's London is too often a limited London. We put up at a nice West End hotel, we take in the Abbey and St. Paul's, maybe the National Gallery and a section or two of the vast British Museum. We watch the guard change at Buckingham Palace *and* the Admiralty (priding ourselves on being inordinately thorough in the realm of spit-and-polish). And damned if we don't have tea at Fortnum's fountain, and perhaps a chophouse dinner. London is cashmere sweaters, a bit of Wedgwood or Royal Derby, and more theater than we take in for the rest of the year—and then some—back home. Upon our return, all that changes are the names of the plays. We're back at Selfridges on Oxford Street (Knightsbridge and emporia like Harrods remain *terra incognita* for masses of us), and we may go so far afield as the Impressionists at the Courtauld in Bloomsbury, or to Windsor Castle.

My point is that there is so very much more that is so very accessible. In no major city of the planet is veering from the beaten path—and believe me, I am all for the beaten path for starters—more pleasurable or more rewarding. My earliest London visits were as a student up for weekends from Southampton University in Hampshire; they were quite as stereotyped as those I delineate above. But some years back, I vowed to take in new places each time I returned, which has been often. I became a museum-church-stately home-shop-restaurant-pub-hotel-excursion nut. I got about by foot (only New York, Paris and Buenos Aires rank with London as walking cities) whenever possible, and alternatively by Underground, bus and taxi in that order.

These pages are a consequence. All in all, a quarter-century of London-looking has gone into this book. It is not unlike the eight earlier volumes of my A to Z series in that it is unabashedly subjective on a number of counts. The most important are what is included and what is not. I devote a lot of space to things to see and places to go. I am not now and never have been of the school that discourages popping into churches and museums and old houses on the shockingly specious grounds that if you've seen one, you have seen the lot.

On the other hand, I have worked hard at researching creature comforts, for I confess to as passionate an interest in this area as in the more profound aspects of the travel experience. I'm not happy if the hotel in which I am staying disappoints or if restaurants are substandard. There are, therefore, a substantial quantity of evaluations of hotels—modest, middling and grand—that I have either lived in, eaten and drunk at, or quite thoroughly inspected; of a wide gamut of restaurants—again in all price ranges from cheap-snack to quite splendid, with the majority in the middle category and with varying types of cuisines, too. There's a section on atmospheric pubs for both solid and liquid nourishment. And on London after dark: the legitimate theaters, of course. But London is no slouch in any of the performing arts—opera and ballet, symphonic orchestras and choral concerts, mod and rock, the London-invented discothèque and other aspects of a well-developed night life that is more ingrained in the British life-style than many visitors suspect.

I start out in this book, as in its predecessors, with a bit of background—enough, I hope, to whet the newcomer's appetite, by providing a brief fill-in on what has gone before in the couple of millennia since the Romans came north and transformed the Celts' Lyndin into the Latin Londinium. Then the nitty-gritty: from a geographic orientation, through my own dozen basic London requisites, into the various Londons as I see them— Architectural (an alphabetical sampler from Bank of England to University of London), Ecclesiastical (churches by Wren and Gibbs and by Gothic and Victorian architects as well), Museum-goer's (reports on what I consider the two dozen most visit-worthy), Verdant (the too-often underappreciated parks and squares) and Peripheral (this last embraces visits to easy-to-reach stately homes on the very fringe of town).

A selection of day-long excursions into the countryside follows —from Bath in the west to Canterbury in the east, Cambridge in the north to Salisbury in the south. There is a major chapter on shops that I've scouted, divided alphabetically into a score of categories, not excluding all of the major department stores and the street markets that are so distinctive to London.

Well, then. I've given you an idea of how I look at London and how I—presumptuous foreigner that I am—attempt to in-terpret it, from, say, Sir Chistopher Wren (there's a biographical sketch in Chapter 2 of this builder-genius who never trained as an architect) to newspapers and magazines (they're appraised in Chapter 7). What I write least about are the Londoners themselves. They are there, along with their city and its institu-tions, for each of us to get to know on his own terms. They do not always profess to understand our fascination with their town. But they invariably welcome us sincerely and, frequently, wittily. Coupled with the setting for this kind of hospitality, we have no right, as visitors, to ask any more.

Robert S. Kane

1 London: To Know

It may well be that London has always tried harder because it is an island city, physically detached from the larger Continent, and anxious to prove that the English Channel and the North and Irish seas were quite the reverse of barriers to its development. Your Londoner today is neither aggressive nor restless nor impatient. But surely his forebears must have been. Else how would such a great and beautiful and, for long, powerful city have evolved on a dampish, northern island?

THE NAME'S THE THING

Not that London was without certain advantages. A head start for one. And a name that stuck, for another. The Celts—poets then, as now—were calling the place Lyndin—a name with a nice ring to it that meant waterside fortress—as long ago as the first century of the Christian era, when the Roman legions happened up from France to settle in. Always better at adapting than originating, they simply Latinized Lyndin to Londinium.

There was a brief period, not long after their arrival, when it was touch and go whether they could stay. The Celts' own queen, Boadicea by name, tried to oust the rascals from the fort they had built. But to no avail. Roman walls went up, Roman laws were introduced, the Roman culture, and the Latin language; all had been implanted by the time of the Roman exodus four hundred years later.

There followed that confusing, albeit alliterative run of the

"E" kings—Egbert and Ethelwulf and Ethelbald and Ethelbert and Ethelred and Edmund and Edred and Edwy and Edgar. Until Alfred the Great—no one has explained his refreshingly distinctive name—none of this "E" crowd was especially London-oriented. Alfred changed all this. He chose London as his capital, which was an achievement in itself. But he was, as well, a pursuer of peace in an age when war was the norm.

Additionally, he set his people's sights on education and literacy, first setting up a school for his largely illiterate nobles, and second, ordering translated the handful of important books of the time from Latin—still the literary tongue of his realm—to English. After settling in, he gave London its first proper government.

1066 AND ALL THAT

London then was the easterly sector of what all these subsequent centuries has been called the City—which continues to jealously guard its independence of the rest of London. Its government was such that with the invasion of England by William the Conqueror in 1066, the City of London was treated with separately, allowing its citizens to democratically elect their officials, as they had since Alfred's time. The Tower of London —or at least the White Tower, its nucleus—went up during William's time.

But just before then, William's predecessor and boyhood chum, the sainted Edward the Confessor, had begun to personally supervise the building of Wesminster Abbey to replace an earlier church that had been on the site. It was Edward, with his attention to the Abbey at Westminster, who succeeded in transferring the Court and government from the Tower area of the City to Westminster—where it has remained for almost a millennium, with hardly a break.

All the while, under later kings like Richard I (who gave the City the Lord Mayor and corporation form of government it has never abandoned) and Henry III (who built still another Westminster Abbey—the one we know today), London continued to expand, economically as well as architecturally and politically.

The medieval centuries saw the craft and trade guilds become important. Lawyers formed their still-extant—and still eminently visitable—Inns of Court.

HENRY VIII: SIX WIVES, THREE CHILDREN

At mid-point in the mid-fifteenth century, England had spent a hundred fruitless years fighting to retain her French territory, to no avail. The ugly civil strife with the beautiful name— Wars of the Roses—between Yorks and Lancasters, followed, with Henry VII's victory at Bosworth Field, and then the eventful reign of his son, Henry VIII. Political turmoil, war, disease —nothing stopped London's growth. Although Holbein and other painters had to be imported from the Continent, there was no dearth of domestic architects or artisans.

Henry VIII's reign saw Hampton Court erected, as but one of many Tudor-style forerunners of later Renaissance building. It was Henry VIII, of course, whose complex marital situation led to the break with the Roman Catholic Church and the establishment of the Church of England. The religious schism resulting was to trouble England for many successive reigns.

Three of Henry's half-dozen wives bore him children, and each reigned: the bright but sickly youngster, Edward VI, for half a decade; the bitterly unhappy Bloody Mary for still another half-decade, which was marked by her disastrous marriage to Catholic Spain's Philip II and a wholesale massacre of Protestant subjects thereafter; and then Elizabeth I—the spinster Elizabeth, during whose forty-five years on the throne England became a world power to be reckoned with. Elizabeth resumed the Protestantism of her father over the fanatic Catholicism of her half-sister. Elizabeth's fleet defeated the great Spanish Armada of her ex-brother-in-law and spurned suitor, Philip II. Elizabeth's knights—Raleigh was, of course, but one—secured the colonial empire of the New World.

THE FIRST ELIZABETH'S ENGLAND

It was Elizabeth's reign that produced Shakespeare, Marlow, Spenser, Bacon, Drake. The Renaissance architecture of these years took its name from the Queen; these were the decades of the great Elizabethan country houses like Knole and Kent and Moreton Hall; of sprouting new colleges at both Oxford and Cambridge; of elaborate formal gardens setting off the manors and palaces; and of design that formed the basis of the succeeding reign. Jacobean—named for James I—is best typified by Hatfield House, the manor that went up on the grounds of an earlier, smaller house where Elizabeth succeeded to the throne; it was followed by the Renaissance style of the remarkable Inigo Jones.

The son of the ill-fated Mary Queen of Scots (whom Elizabeth imprisoned and beheaded), already James VI of Scotland, succeeded Elizabeth as James I of England. We know him best for his still-used version of the Bible. He ushered in a troubled era. Charles I, his successor, was so disliked by Parliament that it tried him for high treason and then chopped his head off. (You may see a statue of him in Whitehall not far from where he was beheaded.) The bleak, stern Commonwealth of the Cromwells, father Oliver and son Richard, followed—but only for a decade. Charles II (in the company of orange-vending Nell Gwynn—perhaps the most celebrated of his mistresses) effected the spirited Restoration—not as lavish, perhaps, as the contemporary France of Louis XIV, but one that put London in high spirits, completely unprepared for the tragedy of the plague that killed off a third of its citizens, only to be cruelly followed by the Great Fire that razed almost the whole of the City. A young inventor and astronomer—not trained as an architect—named Sir Christopher Wren, designed a new St. Paul's Cathedral as a memorial to the old one claimed by the Great Fire. A prolific, long-lived genius, Wren's many works included half a hundred City churches, more than half a hundred additional churches, inspiring an entire school of followers, who created much of the London of ensuing decades.

THE FURNITURE MONARCHS: ANNE, WILLIAM AND MARY

The Catholic-Protestant confusion engendered by Henry VIII continued, even now, to influence the choice of occupants for the throne, to the point where Catholic James II was booted out, and Protestant Dutchman Prince William of Orange was called across the North Sea to reign with his English wife, Mary, one of the two Protestant daughters of the deposed James II. The second daughter, Anne, followed William and Mary to the throne and had more success giving her name to the handsome Renaissance school of furniture and design that sprouted over England than to giving birth to an heir—or even heiress. Poor Anne, who reigned only a dozen years, was pregnant seventeen times by her rather simple, albeit good-natured, Danish husband, but only one child lived, to die a young eleven.

Anne, like her predecessors, William and Mary, lived away from the center of town, mainly in the palace at Kensington, part of which is now the home of Princess Margaret and the Earl of Snowdon, and part of which is open to the public. (Anne moved about though, to ancient Windsor and Hampton Court in summer, and to St. James's Palace in town, as well as Kensington in winter. She never visited Scotland as Queen, although the important Act of Union between England and Scotland came about during her reign.) Anne was so proud of the Duke of Marlborough's victories over the French that she built Blenheim Palace for him as a gift from the nation. (The duke's wife, Duchess Sarah, was Anne's great friend while he was away fighting England's battles, but the two—Sarah and Anne—parted enemies.) Blenheim Palace, now a major excursion destination out of London, was, several centuries later, the birthplace of Winston Churchill.

THE TEUTONIC-ORIGIN FOUR GEORGES

German relatives—the easy-to-remember four Georges—succeeded heirless Anne on the throne. Of these, only the last two were especially interesting: The long-reigning George III, because of his repressive policies, lost England its non-Canadian colonies in North America; and George IV, because, while Prince Regent during his father's latterly insane years, he commissioned a genius named John Nash to build what we now term Regency London. What Wren did for Renaissance London, Nash did for the capital of the early nineteenth century, with Regent's Park, Regent Street, Waterloo Place, and Carlton House Terrace. (Alas, "Prinny's" Carlton House—his town palace—is no more. But his Royal Pavilion at Brighton—a prime excursion destination out of London—is as enchanting as ever it was.)

EIGHTEENTH-CENTURY BRILLIANCE

The city had not, to be sure, stagnated during the eighteenth century, which saw the construction of Grosvenor, Hanover, Bedford, and Soho squares and which was, after all, the great era of Georgian architecture and applied arts ranging from silver to furniture. The great Inigo Jones (whose Whitehall Banqueting House is a requisite London destination) introduced the neoclassic Palladian into London from Italy, and the great Robert Adam later became its chief practitioner in Edinburgh as well as London, not to mention Bath. Cabinetmakers with immortal names like Chippendale, Sheraton, Hepplewhite, and the multi-talented William Kent, created the beautiful furniture for the elegant Georgian houses. Slender-spired colonnaded churches—James Gibbs's St. Martin's-in-the-Fields in London's Trafalgar Square is a prime example—went up in profusion. And the style found great favor in the American colonies, where we still often refer to Georgian houses and churches—as well as latter-day adaptations like banks and schools—as "colonial."

English painters came into their own—late, if contrasted with the Continent—but great: William Hogarth, Sir Joshua Reynolds, Sir Thomas Lawrence and those other painters of beautiful English ladies and beautiful English landscapes: Thomas Gainsborough and George Romney, not to mention Scottish Sir Henry Raeburn.

VICTORIA'S SIXTY-FOUR-YEAR REIGN

Victoria—a niece of the brothers George IV and William IV, and a granddaughter of George III—ascended the throne in 1837 and stayed there—much of the time in mourning at Windsor for Albert, her German-born husband, who died in 1861—until 1901. Her reign of sixty-four years was the longest in English history, and saw England evolve into a democratic nation during a long, mostly peaceful era. Victorian London is to be seen at every turn—the City is full of the heavily proportioned construction of the era, with its penchant for the neo-Gothic.

But so much else bears the name of that long-reigning lady: furniture, interiors, fiction, and hardly the least, morals. This was the age when Britain consolidated her far-flung empire, and even the late-twentieth-century traveler is not allowed to forget it. My National Geographic Atlas lists nearly three-score Victorias around the world, ranging from the capitals of British Columbia, the Seychelles, and Hong Kong, to the falls of the Zambezi River dividing Zambia from Rhodesia, the territory on the map designated Victoria Land, Antarctica; a state in Australia; a creek in Alaska; a beach in Manitoba; a fjord in Greenland; a harbor in Ontario; a river (the Victoria Nile) in Uganda; a point with capital P in Burma; just plain towns in Illinois, Kansas, Texas, and Virginia (only one of which states, incidentally, is a one-time British colony).

Victoria reigned for so long that her portly heir, Edward VII, was sixty when he acceded, along with his breathtakingly beautiful—albeit hard of hearing—Queen, Alexandra, daughter of Denmark's King Christian IX. His reign was short—just under a decade—but still it constituted an era, and not as giddy an era as we have been led to believe. Edward VII never gets quite the credit he deserves for his diplomatic talents. He was an intelligent man, and his tact and brain had a lot to do with the development of cordial Anglo-French relations, which were to prove so valuable in World War I.

Britain emerged a victor from that conflict, and the decades before World War II saw—among a lot else—the very proper reign of George V (almost a dead ringer for his contemporary cousin Nicholas II, the last of the Russian emperors) and the formidable Queen Mary, as well as the first Labor government under Ramsay MacDonald, and the abdication that the world has never stopped talking about: that of the globally popular, brand-new-to-the-throne Edward VIII, who became the Duke of Windsor, and the husband of a twice-divorced American, Mrs. Wallis Warfield Simpson.

CHURCHILL AND THE CURRENT ELIZABETHAN ERA

World War II was Britain's darkest yet bravest hour. Following Nazi Germany's invasion of Poland in 1939, Britain entered the war. The coalition government of Winston Churchill led it to victory, although after the invasion and occupation of France in 1940 it fought alone, until joined by the United States at the end of 1941. London suffered from repeated World War II bombings. Great portions of it were blitzed, and many of its people were killed or wounded.

No people were braver than Londoners during World War II, and at no era in history were the British and American peoples closer than during World War II and the immediate post-World War II years. Chances are that the Underground platform at which you wait for a train was slept upon by countless Londoners in the course of almost nightly air raids. (The extraordinary depth of the underground stations—many twice as far down as are those of, say, New York—were a major factor in saving many lives.)

The well-liked wartime king, George VI, was a postwar casualty. He died in 1952, and his elder daughter, Princess Elizabeth (born 1926) became Queen Elizabeth II while animal-viewing in the bush lodge called Treetops during an official visit to Kenya. (You read a bronze plaque to that effect on the Treetops terrace, while you sip your afternoon tea in the company of a gregarious family of baboons, who come each afternoon to be fed hot scones.) Elizabeth and her husband, Prince Philip, the Duke of Edinburgh—a former Greek prince and nephew of Lord Mountbatten, the last British viceroy of India—have four children; the Princes Edward (born 1964) and Andrew (born 1960), Princess Anne (born 1950), and the eldest and heir apparent, Charles, Prince of Wales (born 1948.) Princess Anne became the bride of Captain Mark Phillips in 1973, the first of the Queen's children to marry. Other immediate members of the Royal Family are Queen Elizabeth the Queen Mother (born 1900), widow of George VI, and the Scottish-born daughter of the 14th Earl of Strathmore and Kinghorne; Princess Margaret (born 1930), the Queen's sister and sole sibling, whose husband is the Earl of Snowdon, formerly Antony Armstrong-Jones (their children are Viscount Linley and Lady Sarah Armstrong-Jones); and the Duke and Duchess of Gloucester—the duke is the Queen's only living uncle on her father's side.

But there are still other Royal Family members. The visitor to London will learn of their comings and goings frequently, in the newspapers and glossy magazines, and on televison. They include the surviving son of the Duke and Duchess of Gloucester, Prince Richard of Gloucester (whose brother, William, died as a result of a 1972 air crash); the children of the late Duke and Duchess of Kent—the present Duke and his Duchess, his sister, Princess Alexandra, and her husband, Angus Ogilvy; and his brother, Prince Michael of Kent. There are, as well, the children of the late Princess Royal (sister of the Queen's father), the Earl of Harewood (whose divorce from his first wife was a Royal Family "first") and his present countess, and the earl's younger brother, Gerald Lascelles.

Following the Royal Family, on the social scale, is the hereditary peerage, embracing (along with their families, many of whose members have lesser titles) 26 dukes, 200 earls, nearly 500 barons, 132 viscounts, and a larger numbers of baronets, who are addressed as "Sir," as also are knights, who are granted their titles only for their own lifetimes in recognition of distinctive services of one sort or another to the nation. Knights are only a part of the nearly 700 Honors Lists recipients given annually by the government and ranging from titled lifetime (non-hereditary) barons to recipients of the Order of the British Empire and Companion of the British Empire, who are identified by initials following their names (O.B.E., C.B.E.) rather than titles preceding them. Additionally, there are honors bestowed by the sovereign acting without the advice of the government. These include the Knights of the Garter and (for Scots) the Thistle, and the coveted, rarely bestowed Order of Merit.

LATE TWENTIETH-CENTURY LONDON

London's oldest and most historic sector, the earlier-described City area, has been self-governing, with its own Lord Mayor and Corporation, since it was founded, in medieval times. The Lord Mayor is invariably a merchant or industrialist with enough wealth and leisure to be able to afford to make frequent ceremonial appearances in public (the annual Lord Mayor's dinner is a major London event). He is aided in governing by a couple of dozen additional aldermen, 159 councilmen and a pair of sheriffs, all of whom work with the guilds, or livery companies, whose origins go back more than half a millennium. There are more than eighty guilds, and of these a favored dozen are officially designated "great." They carry considerable prestige and include the Mercers', Grocers', Drapers', Fishmongers', Goldsmiths', and Haberdashers' guilds.

The City continues to run its own police department (its bobbies have distinctive red-and-white sleeve insignia), and is not unlike New York's Wall Street area in that it is virtually deserted by night with but a few thousand residents, in contrast to the half-million plus who labor in the area by day—many of them eternally dressed in the traditional dark-suit "uniforms" topped by the derby hats that are known as bowlers in England, and never, ever without tightly rolled umbrellas.

The rest of London is something else again. Its oldest sector is Westminster, the area that developed around the Abbey and that took its name because of its position west of the City. By the late nineteenth century the London area was a confusing complex of political entities, and in 1888 the lot joined forces as the County of London, to be governed by the London County Council. Ancient Westminster later achieved status as a city—but within the London County apparatus.

Much more recently, in 1965, Greater London came into being, with an area of 620 square miles—extending beyond the old County of London into Hertfordshire, Surrey, Kent, Essex and Middlesex, embracing this last-named county completely; with a population close to eight million, and under the aegis of a new government agency, the Greater London Council. (In contrast, the City embraces but one square mile, with a resident population of 4,500.)

Included in contemporary Greater London are thirty-two boroughs, each governed at the local level by a mayor and a council, with the GLC's administration in the hands of its Chairman, who is, in effect, the mayor of the world's largest-in-area municipality, with an annual operating budget of some $2.5 million—and its enterprises correspondingly greater than those of most UN member countries. The GLC operates out of County Hall, a massive nineteen-twenties block on the north bank of the Thames, near Westminster Bridge, and just opposite Festival Hall. Its governing body is comprised of a hundred councilors and sixteen aldermen who elect a chairman from among their ranks, and represent the various boroughs, deliberating on alternate Tuesday afternoons, with sessions open to the public.

If Britain has come full circle in this second Elizabethan era, so has its capital. It was during the reign of the first Elizabeth that the Empire became great, with London assuming international dominance, both commercial and political. It has been during the reign of the second Elizabeth that the Empire has been largely dismantled. The overwhelming majority of the colonies around the world—the invincible Empire on which the sun never set—are now mostly sovereign republics voluntarily—purely voluntarily—associated with the Commonwealth of Na-

tions. All told, the Commonwealth has thirty-two members, ranging from old-timers like Australia and Canada to relative newcomers like Tonga and the Bahamas. Of the thirty-two, twenty-
two are republics; ten remain monarchies, governed by their
own prime ministers but with Queen Elizabeth II doubling as
their head of state, as well as the head of state of the United
Kingdom.

Regardless of the nature of the association of their govern-
ments with Whitehall and the Crown, London remains a formidable lure to substantial segments of the population of every
Commonwealth country, just as English remains the *lingua franca*
of each—varied nationalist linguistic sentiments notwithstanding.
If the Commonwealth helped make London one of the most
cosmopolitan of capitals, then the Continent will make it even
more so. For within decades of the loss of Empire, came membership in the Common Market, an association whose internationalist
ramifications are only just beginning to be appreciated. Of *course*
there will always be an England—and a London as its capital.

2 *London: To See*

The beauty of London comes through from the window of one's
sedate black taxi, from the moment of arrival: the campanile of
Big Ben and the tower of Parliament over the Thames, Victorian
grandeur and Georgian elegance, Regency terraces and Renaissance palaces. A further glance or two reveal the polished brass
of Mayfair and its glossy shops, churches by Wren and Gibbs
and the Gothic cathedrals, department stores unsurpassed in style
or luxury by those of any other city, pageantry that is positively
medieval in its splendor, bus conductors who are earthily Cockney, warmly Caribbean, sedately Indian.

London's geography—that is a slower matter. It takes longer
to master. It requires memorization, and then lots of footwork,
despite the enormity of the area involved. Don't worry about
mastering the complexity of the manifold boroughs of the entity
known as Greater London. What primarily interests most visitors
is the West End and the City, contiguous areas on the north
side of the Thames. Look at your map and let me try to orient
you very broadly.

Start in Piccadilly Circus, the best-known if hardly the best-
looking of London's squares. This is the core of the visitor's West
End. Almost due north is Regent Street, with its great stores.
Almost east is Shaftesbury Avenue, worth remembering because
it leads to the maze of legitimate theaters which are a prime
London lure, and to the foreign restaurants of Soho.

Walk south on an extension of Regent Street or on Haymarket, running parallel to it, and you are in the ancient St. James's area. The first major cross street is smart cab-lined Pall Mall, and one walks east on it to enormous Trafalgar Square, with its elegant fountains, towering Nelson Column, and such other landmarks as the National Gallery, National Portrait Gallery, and Church of St. Martin's-in-the-Fields.

Walk through the square, continuing east to the Strand. In just a few blocks it changes its name to Fleet Street, at once newspaper center of the country and the beginning of the original, still separately governed, City area, the economic and financial center of the Commonwealth, with its major landmarks the high-domed St. Paul's Cathedral; the busy area around Threadneedle Street, site of the Bank of England and the Royal Exchange; the tranquil legal oases that are the Inns of Court; and the Thames-front Tower of London.

The Strand is as good a place as any to cross one of the many bridges leading over the Thames to South London; Waterloo Bridge leads one to the modern Royal Festival Hall, and just beyond, Waterloo Station. If one went farther east, the crossing could be made on London Bridge, with Gothic Southwark Cathedral just over the water.

Return now to where we started, Piccadilly Circus. Walk directly west on the broad thoroughfare known as Piccadilly. Within a few blocks, just beyond the Royal Academy of Arts, you will come to a street running perpendicular to Piccadilly, in a northerly direction. It is fashionable Bond Street. You may walk it due north until you come to the major intersecting artery called Oxford Street—a major shopping thoroughfare with middle-category shops and department stores including the giant Selfridges.

Return, now, to Piccadilly, and continue walking west. The park on your left is Green Park. Contiguous with it are Buckingham Palace Gardens, with Buckingham Palace overlooking them; and St. James's Park. The most impressive approach to the palace is via The Mall, a handsome artery cutting through St. James's and Green parks, and passing by a cluster of Royal Palaces—St. James's, Marlborough House, Clarence House, and the once-royal Lancaster House.

Return once again to Piccadilly. Continue walking along it until it terminates at Park Lane. Turn right onto Park Lane and walk along it to the north. The park it is named for is Hyde Park, which it fronts. Park Lane is the locale of a number of fine hotels and it is the western frontier of Mayfair, whose maze of charming streets provides the stuff of limitless exploration. Still another major park—Regent's, with its remarkable zoo—is way to the north of Mayfair. Kensington—where many visitors live and which all want to at least partially explore—lies to the south of Hyde Park, and Knightsbridge (dominated by Harrods department store), Belgravia and Chelsea—all fashionable—border it, stretching to Cheyne Walk and the Chelsea Embankment on the Thames.

For the rest, one does well to walk, good map in hand, as frequently and incessantly as possible, and to memorize—London is too illogical, geographically, to be learned any other way—from frequent references to maps. After a while, one realizes that a saving grace in the town's make-up is the prevalence of squares, with the major ones—and the structures thereon—excellent landmarks and direction-finders. There are, for example, Grosvenor and Berkeley squares in Mayfair, Sloane and Cadogan squares in Chelsea; Belgrave and Eaton squares in Belgravia; Russell, Bedford and Bloomsbury squares in Bloomsbury, near the British Museum and the University of London; Portman, Manchester and Cavendish squares near Wigmore Street just north of the important Oxford Street thoroughfare, and in the City, the green, campuslike Inns of Court—Gray's, Lincoln's, and the Temple.

Important, too, are major streets that border the parks—Bayswater Road, Park Lane, Kensington Road and Kensington Church Street—encircling contiguous Kensington Gardens and Hyde Park; Piccadilly, forming the northern boundary of Green Park and leading to the landmark that is Hyde Park Corner. And after a while, one senses the strategic situation of such major thoroughfares as Knightsbridge and—leading from it—Sloane Street and Brompton Road; Regent Street, running from Oxford Street to Piccadilly Circus; Charing Cross Road, leading from Oxford Street to Trafalgar Square; Ludgate Hill and Cannon Street—extensions of the Strand/Fleet Street in the City; Victoria

Street, which cuts through Westminster; King's and Fulham roads, both major Chelsea streets.

Still another aid to the newcomer: street signs. After Paris, London is the best street-marked of the world's great cities. If it is not quite as label-compulsive as Paris (which to its great credit puts signs over the tiniest and shortest alleys), it is way, way ahead of New York and of such Continental oldies as Rome. And the signs invariably tell you not only the name of the street, but of the borough and its directional (W. 1, S.W. 2) designation.

THE ESSENTIAL LONDON: A DOZEN REQUISITES

The newcomer to a strange city—especially a *large,* strange city, feels nothing if not inadequate. There can be moments, shortly after checking into one's hotel, after clothes are hung up and the bellman tipped, when nothing would be more appealing than home, sweet home. Where, oh where, and how, oh how, to begin to tackle such a formidably immense urban area? Kane's first self-rule, which I impose upon myself in any new place: Get out of that hotel room, and *quickly.* Even an aimless, destinationless stroll is better than half a wasted forenoon or afternoon in Room 712, color telly or no. As for the manner of tackling, here, in the case of London, is one enthusiast's personally compounded prescription: the twelve absolutely basic and requisite attractions, almost guaranteed to make a London fan, if not a neo-Londoner, out of a skeptical newcomer.

The National Portrait Gallery (St. Martin's Lane at Trafalgar Square, just behind the National Gallery): I often wish that my first destination on my first trip to London had been the National Portrait Gallery. Its concept is such a brilliant one that the Scots have adapted it in Edinburgh, and they do not often emulate their English cousins so obviously. The purpose is to give one an idea of what Britain has been all about, these many centuries, by means of portraits of its leading personalities—not only kings, queens and royal mistresses, as important as they have been, heaven knows, but politicians, writers, poets, scientists, and musi-

cians. You'll find the works of such painters as Sir Peter Lely and
Sir Godfrey Kneller—the German-born portraitists who rose to
eminence in Charles II's court—and of later English masters like
Reynolds, Romney and Lawrence, and of many foreign painters,
too. On two recent visits, the museum was passing out a folder
"intended for the visitor with only a limited period of time at
his disposal." It suggested viewing these "Six Famous Portraits in
Fifteen Minutes": Sir Walter Raleigh by Nicholas Hilliard;
Queen Elizabeth I by Gheeraedts the Younger; Henry VIII by
—of course, you know—Holbein; Shakespeare by an unknown
artist; that superbly gossipy Restoration diarist, Samuel Pepys,
by John Hayls; and the remarkably talented Brontë girls—
Charlotte, Emily and Anne—by their brother, Branwell.

But these are but a handful. There is the unkind, unflatter-
ing, portrait of Elizabeth II, painted in 1970 by Annigoni; one
can but admire Her Majesty for allowing its display. There is a
fine Robert Walker study of Cromwell which well portrays his
stern prudery. There is the great Kneller portrait of Sir Christopher
Wren, a typically voluptuous Peter Lely of Charles II's favorite
mistress, Nell Gwyn (who, with her bulging eyes, sensuous red lips
and flowing brown curls, does not look much different from the
many other ladies Lely painted).

The famous Phillips painting of Lord Byron got up in Greek
costume, with a wispy mustache that looks as if it had been
pasted on, is at the gallery. And so, in contrast, are Victorian
ministers like Melbourne and Peel, Georgian theater folk like
Sheridan and Sarah Siddons. Gets you in the mood, sets the
stage: that's what the National Portrait Gallery does. And very
well indeed.

Tower of London: If the Tower, to use the vernacular, is not
quite where it's all at, it is surely where it all began. To term it
the major remaining souvenir of medieval London is to understate. William the Conqueror founded the Tower almost a millennium ago, and succeeding sovereigns took up where he left
off. No single London locale is more history-drenched, for the
Tower has served as military citadel, royal residence, political
prison, mint, observatory, and repository of royal property rang-

ing from precious documents to crown jewels. Not all of these functions are contemporary, to be sure, but even today the Tower remains, nominally at least, a royal palace under the direct control of the sovereign.

It is, as well, a functioning garrison, under the command of a Crown-appointed Constable (usually a retired soldier of distinction, who does not live within its precincts) and a Governor (who has the privilege of calling home the Queen's House, a handsome Tudor mansion in the Tower complex). The troops under the Governor's command are, of course, the Yeoman Warders. Their usual uniform is of blue and is relatively somber, but they are best known (thanks in modern times to a gin called Beefeater) by the brilliant red, black and gold outfits, with Elizabethan white ruffs round their necks, that date back to the mid-sixteenth century. They are all mature men, for to become a yeoman warder, one must have been not only a sergeant in one of the military services, but a recipient of the Good Conduct or Long Service medal as well.

The major building within the complex is the White Tower, so called because it was originally whitewashed. It was home to a long line of medieval kings; they lived on the top floor, conducted business in the council chamber just below, and worshiped in the beautiful St. John the Evangelist Chapel, which has been the setting for a good deal more than ordinary worship services; Mary I—Bloody Mary—was married by proxy in the chapel to Spain's Philip II, not too many years before her half-sister, Elizabeth I, defeated Philip's great Armada and changed the course of history.

You'll want also to see the rather aptly named Bloody Tower— one must give the British credit for not being squeamish in the official designation for this structure—for it was where the ghoulish sixteenth-century royal murders occurred. Either Richard III or Henry VII was the culprit, depending upon which version of history one goes along with, and the victims were the young princes, Edward V and the Duke of York. The Crown Jewels, of recent years, repose in the contemporary sub-surface Jewel House, the better to preserve them. They comprise a quite literally dazzling assortment of orbs, scepters, swords and, of course, crowns with the range from Edward the Confessor to Queen Mother Elizabeth—or, in other words, about a thousand years. There remains the Chapel Royal of St. Peter ad Vincula, a Tudor treasure, at whose Sunday morning services the public is cordially welcome.

Westminster Abbey—or the Minster in the west, as contrasted to St. Paul's and the Tower in the City to the east—is the core of the "new" London, that area which the court, government and church developed at the time of Edward the Confessor, a millennium ago. The Abbey is peculiar in that it is not actually an abbey (monks have not been resident since the time of the first of the three structures on the site), and that it is not a cathedral (for it is not the seat or *cathedra* of the bishop of a diocese, St. Paul's having that distinction for London, and distant Canterbury Cathedral, for all of England). Neither is it an ordinary parish church.

It is, instead, designated a "royal particular" and it has become, over the centuries, a kind of national history book in a Gothic cover. There is no denying its architectural distinction. It goes back to the mid-thirteenth century (a joint effort of Edward the Confessor and Henry III), and its elongated, splendidly high nave—despite the jarring presence of the inappropriate crystal chandeliers that illuminate it, and an early Victorian choir screen—is among the handsomest in England. So, for that matter, is the choir, even though much of it is surprisingly modern. There are fine tombs—Eleanor of Castile's is a standout—and there are other nooks and crannies and corners and vistas that are esthetically, let alone spiritually, moving. The Abbey is historically fascinating—monarch after monarch (including Elizabeth I and her adversary, Mary Queen of Scots) is buried within, and so are poets and politicians and war heroes, there being a chapel dedicated to Royal Air Force men killed in the World War II Battle of Britain. The fan vaulting of Henry VII's chapel is superb. (It would be even more so without the distracting multicolored flags which protude from its walls.)

But withal, the Abbey comes through, to at least one not infrequent visitor, as too scrubby-uppied, too classroomy, too official. I prefer Southwark across the River, or a Wren—or pre-

Fire—church in the City. But you must make a duty call; after all, every sovereign has been crowned there—on the Coronation Chair that encloses the ancient Stone of Scone—since Edward the Confessor, save two: Edward V, the boy king who was murdered in the Tower in 1483, aged 13; and Edward VIII, the late Duke of Windsor, who reigned for less than a year in 1936, abdicating before his coronation.

The Houses of Parliament are mostly—there are significant exceptions—Victorian, and aside from their importance as the seat of the national legislature—a legislature that once controlled the destiny of great chunks of the world's territory—they represent, at least to me, Victorian architecture and interior design at their most sublime. Westminster—or more officially, the Palace of Westminster—is everything that the Parliament of a great nation should be—elaborate, awesome, elegant, monumentally proportioned, splendidly sited on the Thames, and with not one but two substantial landmark towers that unmistakably identify the nation's seat of governmental power.

Westminster is nothing so simple as the neoclassic Capitol in Washington with one house on either side of a central dome. Its oldest component part, Westminster Hall, goes back to the eleventh century and served as a law court until as recently as the last century. With its great beamed Gothic ceiling, it still sees service as a conference site and as the place where monarchs and national heroes lie in state before burial. St. Stephen's Hall is early Victorian, a replica of the ancient structure that had served as the House of Commons for several event-packed centuries. The adjoining sixteenth-century cloister with its fan vaulting is visit-worthy.

Parliament proper takes its bearings from the elaborate Central Lobby; Commons is in one direction, Lords, the other. The lot is open to the public when the houses are not in session, and there are galleries in both houses for visitors; Britons get tickets through their MPs; foreigners either take their chances by waiting in line out in front the day they want to get in, or by making arrangements in advance through such private tour companies as Grosvenor Travel Service (see Chapter 7).

The House of Lords has less power than its opposite number but its quarters are infinitely more attractive. This, after all, is where the Sovereign addresses both houses at the Opening of Parliament; thus, the splendid throne and adjacent Robing Room, Royal Gallery and Prince's Chamber. Commons is simpler for two important reasons. The first is that traditionally the Sovereign has never been welcome within its precincts. The second is that it was bombed out during World War II and had to be rebuilt. The result is a chamber done on traditional lines but with near barnlike severity. Worth noting: Members' benches in Lords are upholstered in red, those in Commons, green. Colors of benches in the upper and lower houses of Parliaments throughout the Commonwealth are identical in color, almost without exception.

The British Museum: Museums in London, in my view, are important enough to warrant an entire section of their own, later on in this book. Here, among the London requisites, I place but two: the earlier-described National Portrait Gallery because it sets the mood for a London visit, and now the British Museum because it is unique among a handful of the world's greatest. It is the most marvelous of the catch-all museums, full of treasures from every corner of what had been the world's greatest empire.

The neoclassic main building, most of which was erected well over a century ago, is not the easiest to find one's way about. It is, indeed, so complicated that the museum includes a big map in the pocket of the guidebook it sells. (You may buy the map separately.) At least as helpful are the guards—kindly oldtimers most of them and of inestimable value in getting you to what you want to see. You may enter the main building at either the principal entrance on Great Russell Street (it's easier if you start out there) or the north door, on Montague Place.

What you are getting into, to give you a rough idea, is a repository with the following departments, each and every one outstanding among the museums of the world: Coins and Medals, Egyptian Antiquities, Greek and Roman Antiquities, Manuscripts, Medieval Antiquities, Oriental Antiquities, Oriental Printed Books and Manuscripts, Printed Books (including globes and maps), Prints and Drawings, and Western Asiatic Antiquities.

For me, the single most spectacular exhibit is the sculpture from the Parthenon in Athens—the so-called Elgin Marbles—that occupy the entire Duveen Gallery and are arranged in frieze form. They were brought to England in the early nineteenth century by the then Earl of Elgin and once inspected (they take time, but it is worthwhile) one understands why the Greeks have never forgiven the English for removing them from their rightful home. I am partial, too, to the King's Library, a sumptuous early nineteenth-century chamber created to house the books of no less a sovereign than George III, and containing such treasures as the Gutenberg Bible, Shakespeare's first folio, first editions of English books you remember from school and college. There's so much more: the text of Magna Carta, exquisite Japanese scrolls and pottery, the Rosetta Stone, Michelangelo drawings, Indian sculpture, mosaics that go back to the Roman occupation of Britain, massive Assyrian sculptures of human-headed animals. And if you can, take a peek at the circular Reading Room, Britain's counterpart of our Congressional Library. **The Museum of Mankind,** in its own home at 6 Burlington Gardens in Mayfair just behind the Royal Academy, is the Ethnography Department of the British Museum, from which it moved in 1970, gaining infinitely more space for its exhibits and a new name in the bargain. This museum is visit-worthy if only because it has the finest specimens on the planet of the matchless art of the old Nigerian kingdom of Benin—not only of wood, but in iron, bronze and ivory as well. There are other exemplary African exhibits—east and north as well as west. But other galleries turn up such delights as Indonesian puppets, Eskimo carvings, Mexican turquoise mosaics, Australian aboriginal bark painting— the lot masterfully displayed. At both the main museum and the Mankind branch, there are first-rate shops for cards, reproductions and catalogues. The main museum has a gloomy restaurant desperately in need of brightening up.

Hampton Court Palace is one of the two out-of-London excursions I include among these dozen requisites. The other is Windsor Castle, and it is touch and go as to which of the two is the more historically important. A strong case could be made for Windsor, but I much prefer Hampton Court architecturally. Begun in the early sixteenth century by Cardinal Wolsey, it became a royal residence when the crafty cardinal—in a vain attempt to remain in Henry VIII's good graces—made a gift of it to his king, whose successors lived in it through the reign of the second George, in the mid-eighteenth century.

The medieval portions, built by Wolsey and Henry VIII, form the bulk of this complex of quadrangles. But there are newer and equally splendid late-seventeenth century additions, which William and Mary had Sir Christopher Wren design. The public has been welcome since Queen Victoria opened the state rooms, but there are a thousand more chambers which make up into a mass of apartments. They are put to good use as "grace and favor" apartments—residences given by the sovereign to the offspring or widows of favored Crown servants. The Renaissance Wren and Tudor Gothic portions of the palace complement each other—oddly, perhaps, but well.

Memorable interiors are the King's Staircase, with murals by an Italian artist imported by Charles II; the Great Hall, with a dazzling Gothic wood ceiling; the also-Gothic Great Watching Chamber; the various monarchs' bedrooms, presence chambers, closets and chapels, and the Wren-created Cartoon Gallery, intended for a set of Rafael works but now decorated with tapestries that are copies of the original Rafaels; the immense kitchens (it is easy to see how Henry VIII developed his gargantuan appetite), the exterior courtyards, both Tudor and Wren, and the gardens, most particularly the Maze, which dates to Queen Anne's time. In summer consider approaching by boat, along the Thames from Westminster Pier—the same way the monarchs went.

Windsor Castle is at once the oldest and largest and the longest continually inhabited of the network of royal residences. It was Queen Victoria's permanent home for the excessive period of mourning extending over decades, following the death of her consort. But her successors continue to frequent Windsor. It has, despite the alterations, additions and changes which would be inevitable in any residence having such a long and affluent roster of residents, retained its essentially Norman facade.

Henry II's Round Tower is little changed from the time when it went up in the twelfth century, not long after William the Conqueror founded Windsor as the final link in a chain of fortresses ringing London. The old Norman walls remain, too, and the elevated position of the complex is in the storybook tradition of walls, towers and battlements. If the castle's interiors are not as consistent in style as its facade, they are hardly without interest. One may inspect the State Apartments daily throughout the year, except when the Royal Family is occupying them, which is usually during April, parts of June and December.

My favorite rooms are the Queen's Presence Chamber, with its Renaissance painted ceiling, Gobelin tapestries, and Grinling Gibbons carvings; the eighteenth-century Grand Reception Room—very French and very grand indeed—and St. George's Hall, a wonderfully proportioned Gothic rectangle hung with portraits of sovereigns who have been members of the Windsor-headquartered Order of the Garter—including a contemporary likeness of Elizabeth II, at the far end above her throne. Exemplary also is St. George's Chapel, Perpendicular Gothic in style and built by Edward IV.

The Castle's neighbor is **Eton College,** the kingdom's pre-eminent boys' school, where the not-to-be-missed attractions are the chapel—another Perpendicular Gothic masterwork—the five-century-old Lower School, the somewhat newer Upper School (an upstart dated 1690), a library full of treasures, including a copy of the first printed Bible, and some early Shakespeare folios; venerable College Hall and its equally old octagonal kitchen; the multi-period Cloisters and the boys themselves, top-hatted as they have been for many generations.

St. Paul's Cathedral: The reputed Wren masterwork is Protestant Britain's answer to Catholic Rome's St. Peter's Basilica. (Wren had visited Rome on his Grand Tour.) St. Paul's is smaller, of course, but this is not to say it even approaches the intimacy of Wren's warm and charming parish churches, any given half-dozen of which I much prefer. Still, one cannot dismiss St. Paul's, crucifix in shape, with its long nave and monumental dome. There is no gainsaying it is a major work, nor that it means a great deal to Britain, to London and, for that matter, to the British people. Its restoration after World War II bombings was an event of the first rank.

Wren's St. Paul's replaces the earlier "Old" St. Paul's, an absolutely enormous Gothic structure that went up in the eleventh century, was surpassed in size only by the cathedrals of Seville and Milan and was, from all accounts, magnificent. The Civil War and a fire in 1561 had taken their toll, and in 1660 Charles II, upon his restoration, set up a Royal Commission to deal with St. Paul's restoration. Sir Christopher Wren came up with a controversial plan to save what remained. But in 1666, the cathedral was totally razed by the Great Fire of London, and Wren produced several brand new designs, one of which, with modifications, was utilized.

By 1697, services were being held in the choir of the new structure. But if St. Paul's was Wren's masterwork, it was also his greatest trial. A faction of MPs determined that work was not progressing rapidly enough and voted to withhold half of Wren's salary until the cathedral was complete. Not until 1711 was he able to petition Queen Anne, then on the throne, to order that he be paid the arrears due him. St. Paul's was completed during the term of office of a single Bishop of London, and moreover, Wren himself lived to see it nearly finished. In 1786, at the age of eighty-six, he was fired as Surveyor General of the kingdom, but he had by then settled into residence in Hampton Court, and made occasional visits into London to inspect his cathedral. He died at the ripe old age of ninety-one and was buried, appropriately enough, in St. Paul's. A tablet above his grave directs the reader, in Latin: "If you seek his monument, look around."

Kensington Palace is still another London landmark with Wren associations—and with William and Mary connections, as well. King William III had Wren make additions and alterations to the place when he took it over in 1689, as a respite from the damper neighborhood of in-town Whitehall, which he considered not at all healthy for a chronic asthmatic like himself. His successor and sister-in-law, Queen Anne, made additional enlargements during her reign, as did Anne's Teutonic successor, George I, who may not have been able to speak English with any fluency, but could communicate well enough to get the gifted William Kent to decorate the interiors with sumptuous painted walls and ceilings.

The parklike gardens without are lovely (they include the Orangery that Queen Anne had built) and there are surprises within, like Queen Victoria's bedroom and nursery. Victoria was born at Kensington, as was Queen Mary, wife of George V, and grandmother of Queen Elizabeth II. (Kensington seemed to spawn strong-willed royal ladies.) Kensington is the only inhabited royal palace in town whose state apartments are visitable, and whenever I have been there, it has been a puzzlement as to how few visitors are attracted to a place so rich in historic associations, not to mention historic decorations and furnishings. Living elsewhere on the premises are Queen Elizabeth II's sister, Princess Margaret, her husband the Earl of Snowdon, and their children, Viscount Linley and Lady Sarah Armstrong-Jones. The London Museum, which for long occupied another part of the palace, now has its own home in the City—in the Barbican.

The Banqueting House, Whitehall, is on this honor list of requisite destinations for three reasons. First, it is so conveniently located that you can easily pop in to visit it in conjunction with a visit to the Changing of the Horse Guards at the Admiralty. Second, it is a place of visual splendor, for its designer was no less an architect-designer than Inigo Jones, and the immense ceiling is the work of no less a painter than Rubens. And third, because it was a part of a royal palace, in the heart of London, it is absolutely riddled with royal associations of import. Preceding it was York House, like Hampton Court a residence of Cardinal Wolsey and, also like Hampton, taken over by Henry VIII, to remain the London royal residence during a number of ensuing reigns.

Old York House burned and Jones was commissioned to build its replacement, which is one of the three Jones works in London. (The other two are the Queen's House at Greenwich, and St. Paul's Church, Covent Garden.) The Banqueting House was

completed in 1622, in time to serve as the spot from which
Charles I walked to nearby gallows and decapitation. Later,
Cromwell moved in, as Lord Protector, remaining until his death
in 1658. It was to Whitehall that Charles II returned after he
was restored to the throne, and it was here, too, that the Dutchman, Prince William of Orange, and his English wife, Mary,
accepted the Crown in 1689. The palace, Banqueting House excepted, burned in 1698, by which time asthmatic William and his
Queen had long since moved to Kensington with its fresher air.
The hall was excellently restored in the 1960s.

Changing of the Guard: The British sovereign traditionally has two
principal guards that are changed daily to musical accompani-
ment, at two locales. The Queen's Guard embraces personnel of
the various regiments of a composite body known as the Guards
Division, all of whom wear vivid red tunics and towering bear-
skin caps, but who are members either of the Scots, Irish, Welsh,
Coldstream or Grenadier Guards, each with their own uniform
variations. They are quartered at Chelsea Barracks, and stand
duty at Buckingham and St. James's palaces and Clarence
House (residence of the Queen Mother). Additionally, until
1973—nocturnally, at least—they guarded the Bank of England
(thus the expression, "Safe as the Bank of England"). The changing of the Queen's Guard takes place daily at Buckingham Palace
at 11:30 A.M.; get there a little early, so you can see.

The other guard of the sovereign is the Queen's Life Guard,
whose personnel come from among the two regiments of the
Household Cavalry—the Blues and Royals, who wear blue tunics
and whose helmets have red plumes; and the Life Guards, with
red tunics and white plumes atop their helmets. Their functions
include serving as personal bodyguards to the sovereign on
spectacular al fresco occasions, and guarding—while mounted on
horseback—the Admiralty, Whitehall, where the changing ceremony takes place daily at 11 A.M. (10 A.M. on Sundays, with a
less spectacular additional ceremony daily at 4 P.M.). The
Household Cavalry live at Hyde Park Barracks in Knightsbridge, and can be seen each morning marching through the park
to the Admiralty. On a recent London visit when I put up at the

Hyde Park Hotel, the guards marching by under my window served as my morning alarm clock each day.

The Food Halls at Harrods: Harrods, one of the planet's better department stores, is dealt with in the department stores section of the chapter on shopping, in later pages. But I am taking the liberty of detaching the Food Halls from the rest of the store and placing them up front here among London requisites. Every time I visit them I am convinced that I am looking at a marvel of London that not as many visitors from abroad know about as should. I suspect I've another reason, too: There could not possibly be such diverse and sophisticated stocks of foodstuffs for sale in a country where the cuisine is too-often reputed to be poor, as is the case with England. By looking at the food department of this store, even the most casual of visitors appreciates that there just has to be a substantial segment of Londoners who know and love good food enough to support this spectacular enterprise.

Harrods, in Knightsbridge, devotes four enormous and contiguous chambers of its main floor to food. Now, visitors from America, of all countries, do not need to be shown another big supermarket. These halls are no such. Self-service is not the rule to begin with. But it is the way in which things are displayed, in great arrangements in a setting of high tiled walls under gracefully arched ceilings that sets Harrods' edibles apart. The fish and seafood areas are perhaps the most imaginative: Dover soles, finnan haddocks and kippers; oysters, cockles and mussels; prawns and crabs and crayfish. But poultry is present in diversity, from run-of-the-mill chicken to Norfolk ducklings and English capons. The meat counters proclaim that "Scotch Beef Is Butchered by Experts, English, French or American Style." The game departments sell quail, partridge and speckled gulls' eggs, as well. There are smoked cod roe, homemade sausage links, a *charcuterie* that Paris might learn from, with quiches, game pies and pâtés. The bakery features elaborate tortes, traditional English cakes, beautiful breads in infinite varieties and textures, and the best jelly doughnuts north of Berlin. Beyond are fresh fruits and vegetables—including a section "From the Markets of Paris"—that are artfully arranged and beautiful to look upon. The Floral Hall turns plants and cut flowers into a minor art. And the wine shop has an astonishing variety of French, German and other European vintages, not to mention domestic whiskies, and gins in abundance.

ARCHITECTURAL LONDON: AN ALPHABETICAL SAMPLER

Of the great cities, none is quite the delightful achitectural mix of many eras, in quite the same way as London. Gothic, Renaissance, Georgian, Regency, Victorian, Edwardian, and yes, our own era, as well: London has them all. The marvel is that even though it is largely an unplanned city, added on to and altered in the course of centuries, it has had an uncanny knack at creating vistas and areas and neighborhoods that are at once harmonious and eminently livable. The square has been a commonplace since the eighteenth century, and reached a pinnacle during the Regency. The town house, from Renaissance times onward, but especially in the Georgian decades, has been surpassed in no other city. The same might be said about the Londoner's skills with trees and grass and shrubbery and flowers. The world makes fun of the urban Englishman's devotion to his garden, but surely Londoners exceed all other big-city dwellers when it comes to horticultural finesse. And parks: Capability Brown replaced the borrowed, formal French designs with the more indigenous, free-flowing style of England; London's parks, big and small, manifest this concept, and are exceptionally choice green retreats.

Not everything in my alphabetical selection below is open to the public; some places are only partially open, and some are no more than monuments of interest to passers-by.

The Bank of England (Threadneedle Street) gives its name—simply The Bank—to the busy City area it dominates, both structurally and as the unique bank that serves both the British government and the private banking industry, which is heavily represented in the neighborhood. The bank itself, though mostly modern and mostly unvisitable to the public, happily retains the one-story wall-like facade that Sir John Soane (whose house, not far distant, is described in the Museum section) designed for it in the early nineteenth century in neoclassic style. Behind is a modern structure, extending eight stories upward, and several into the depths. Only the entrance hall is open to the public.

The Bridges across the Thames are mostly modern and of little esthetic interest. The most famous, the one that was falling down in our childhood nursery rhyme—*London Bridge*—did just that. Or at least its early nineteenth-century successor did. Too venerable to cope with modern traffic, it suffered the indignity of being taken apart and transported piece by piece to Arizona, where it has been reerected as a tourist lure, to be succeeded by a more functional replacement. *Tower Bridge* is a charming neo-Gothic structure dating only to the turn of the last century, with the Tower of London as a backdrop. *Westminster Bridge,* nineteenth century and nondescript, is highly efficient. So, for that matter, is the much newer (pre-World War II albeit romantically named) *Waterloo Bridge.* The view is nice when you find yourself crossing it, en route to or from Royal Festival Hall. And the vista is equally impressive for pedestrians traversing *Southwark Bridge,* as nice a way as any to approach Southwark Cathedral, on the South Bank.

Buckingham Palace is, of course, the sovereign's London home, and a household word throughout the world. (The reigning monarch's other principal residences are Balmoral in Scotland, built by Victoria and traditionally a summer retreat; Sandringham in Norfolk, bought by Edward VII when Prince of Wales; and ancient Windsor Castle, earlier described.) It is named for the Duke of Buckingham and Chandos, who built it in the eighteenth century, selling it to George III in 1761. George IV, the builder Regent-King who is responsible for the lovely look of what remains of Regency London, had his architect John Nash remodel it in the early nineteenth century, with architect Edward Blore amplifying the Nash work. Queen Victoria—who eventually took it over as her town house, even though she always remained partial to Windsor—made changes, as did her grandson, George V, as recently as 1913.

The only parts of the palace open to the public are the Queen's

Gallery and the Royal Mews (see Museums in this chapter). The setting—Buckingham Palace Gardens, an extension of Green and St. James's parks—is exceptionally capacious and little short of inspired when one considers that the palace is in the heart of a great urban center.

Should you ever get invited inside, the rooms to see are the throne-dominated red and gold State Ballroom, where state banquets are held and where the Queen conducts investitures and other ceremonies; the Throne Room, with its frieze of the Wars of the Roses; the Nash-designed Music Room, with a circular dome supported by Corinthian columns; and the White Drawing Room —with gilded plasterwork, yellow draperies, and sumptuous French and Regency furnishings. And there is a chance of a Palace invitation. After all, the guest list for each of the royal garden parties totals 9,000.

Chelsea Royal Hospital (Royal Hospital and Ormond West roads), is one of the anachronisms that make London so interesting. Charles II founded it as a veterans' hospital in the seventeenth century—much like the Louis XIV-established Les Invalides in Paris. It is still another Wren work—and an exceptional one—with additions by Robert Adam, among others.

Every year—in late May or early June—"the nearest convenient Sunday to the birthday (May 29) of his Gracious Majesty King Charles II, Our Royal Founder" (as the printed program puts it) the Hospital observes Founder's Day in its splendid chapel. Preceding the services, the Governor of the Hospital, in plumed hat, reviews the red-coated inmates, called Pensioners, at a parade on the grounds, with the salute usually taken by a military figure of repute; a military band provides martial music. At the Chapel service, there is fanfare by military trumpeters from the Royal Military School of Music, and the prayers include one taken from the 1662 edition of the Book of Common Prayer, that gives thanks "for the Restoration of the Royal Family."

Not every Sunday service at the hospital is this elaborate (I happened to happen upon a Founder's Day service on a recent visit) but the hospital is never without interest. The Great Hall, just opposite the Chapel, is open to visitors, and so is the Council

Chamber, a feature of which is a group of portraits by Sir Peter Lely, Sir Godfrey Kneller and Sir Anthony Van Dyck. There's a museum, too, with historical documents relating to the hospital, and in May, Britain's fanciest horticulture exhibition, the Chelsea Flower Show, takes place on the grounds, with many of the Royal Family and numbers of peers and their ladies at the opening.

Clubs, mostly for gents, but usually with privileges for their ladies, are a tradition that, for better or for worse, the British have exported to the most distant corners of the planet, not excluding non-white ex-colonies where, traditionally, the dark-skinned locals were rarely if ever—heaven forbid!—admitted, except as servants. A case could be made for the role of the club in the dissolution of the Empire; I shall not forget an unavoidable stay at the whites-only English Club, in pre-independence Zanzibar. But suffice it, at this point, to make mention of the locale of a few of the fancier ones, and to admire them their architecture, if not necessarily their exclusivity. St. James's Street, leading from Piccadilly down to St. James's Palace, is the site of a choice trio— the late-eighteenth-century Brooks, and its also venerable across-the-street neighbors, Boodle's and White's. Pall Mall—the name is believed to come from a Restoration game, *paille-maille*— which runs perpendicular with St. James's Street, is almost exclusively clubs—the Reform and the Travellers', both by the same Sir Charles Barry who designed the great Staircase Hall of neighboring Lancaster House; the Oxford and Cambridge, with its largely academic membership (and super roast beef and Yorkshire pudding in its restaurant, if you're invited), and a number of others, from the Conservative at St. James's Street, to the Athenaeum at Pall Mall's other extremity, Waterloo Place. There are a pair of clubs with American memberships: The American Club (95 Piccadilly) and the American Women's Club (1 A Queens Gate).

Downing Street, a narrow thoroughfare that lies between St. James's Park and Whitehall, about midway between the Admiralty and Parliament, with government ministries all about, is most celebrated for the house at No. 10, which has been the home of the vast majority of Prime Ministers since George II offered it to Sir Robert Walpole well over two centuries ago. Within, is the street-floor Cabinet Room. Since Walpole's time, there have been a number of renovations, including one by the noted Sir John Soane, in 1825, and the latest, in the mid-nineteen sixties. No. 10 is not the only noteworthy house on the street. No. 11 is where Chancellors of the Exchequeur live, and No. 12 is the official digs of the Chief Government Whip, a not unimportant parliamentary political leader. None of this trio of houses is open to the public, but a stroll past can yield glimpses of government leaders and their colleagues, or at the very least members of the press waiting for government leaders and their colleagues.

Lambeth Palace (Lambeth Road—on the South Bank of the Thames at Lambeth Bridge) is an absolutely super Middle Ages cluster. It's the official London home of the Archbishops of Canterbury (the top administrators of the Church of England), and has been these many centuries. There's a formidable gate house, an imposing Great Hall and a venerable detached chapel. The problem is open-hours. Double check before you make the trip.

The Law Courts (Strand, just before it becomes Fleet Street) comprises a sprawling rather gloomy Victorian cluster (Her Majesty dedicated them in 1882) and are officially the Royal Courts of Justice. Cases tried are civil and are usually open to visitors; Monday through Friday 10:30 A.M.–1 P.M. and 2 P.M.–6 P.M. (Criminal cases are tried at Old Bailey.)

Lincoln's Inn and the other Inns of Court: Lincoln's Inn (Chancery Lane) is a sanctuary of tranquility in the midst of the City; half an hour's stroll through it is indeed a London treat. It is one of the so-called Inns of Court, which traditionally control the practice of law in England, and which include resident quarters for member-lawyers, as well as educational and other facilities. Lincoln's Inn (not named for our Abraham, but for a medieval Earl of Lincoln) goes back to the fifteenth century. There is a little bookshop near the entrance that sells a charming little guidebook. What you want to see are the Old Hall, built the

year Columbus discovered our shores; the New Hall—late nineteenth century, the big library, opened by Queen Victoria in
1845; and the much older Chapel, an Inigo Jones structure in
perpendicular Gothic, which was consecrated in 1623, with poet-
cleric John Donne (then the Dean of nearby St. Paul's Cathedral
and a Lincoln's Inn alumnus) at the opening service. Few
monarchs have not participated in Lincoln's Inn activity of one
sort or other. And no less than nine prime ministers have been
Lincoln's Inn-ers, from Walpole through to Asquith.

The other Inns of Court are City neighbors of Lincoln's Inn.
Gray's Inn (Holborn) is an also-medieval complex. The Great
Hall, dating to Tudor times, is exemplary, and so are the library,
chapel and gardens. The *Inner and Middle Temples* (Middle
Temple Lane), the remaining two Inns of Court, share the same
complex as well as the noted Temple Church (see Ecclesiastical
London in this chapter). The name derives from the ancient
Knights Templar of the Crusades, who were the original owners
of the quarter which passed to a community of pedagogical bar-
risters some six centuries ago. The Great Hall of each Temple is
its masterwork. Middle's dates from the late sixteenth century
and much of it—including superb glass and paneling—is original.
Inner Temple's Hall is the third on the site, a post-World War II
whose cornerstone was laid by Queen Elizabeth II in 1952.

The London County Hall (Belvedere Road) is perhaps more
important for its function than for its design. It is a monolithic
nine-story, 1,500-room, nineteen-twenties neo-Renaissance pile,
distinguished by a curved colonnaded front. The situation is
Thames-front, just opposite the Royal Festival Hall complex. The
hall is the headquarters of the administrative machinery for the
Greater London Council (see Chapter 1). To see are the octagonal Council Chamber (the council's meetings, usually alternate
Tuesday afternoons, are open to the public) and the Members'
Library and Reading Room.

Mansion House (Mansion House Street) is the Georgian building
that for long has served as the official home of the City of London's Lord Mayor. Its most distinctive feature is a Corinthian

portico, from which incumbents watch parades and make speeches, from time to time. The major public room is the misnamed Egyptian Hall (its design is neoclassic) which seats several hundred for dinners. There is, as well, the minuscule Lord Mayor's Court of Justice, still in session daily, with His Worship or an alderman presiding, and with cells directly belowstairs.

Marble Arch is a detached segment of Buckingham Palace that George IV's John Nash intended originally as the principal gateway. It was not broad enough for the sovereign's coaches to pass through, so it got moved to a less strategic point outside of the palace some years later. Finally, in 1851, during Victoria's reign, it was transplanted to the site where Park Lane and Oxford Street intersect, where it has remained ever since, a major London landmark.

The Monument (Fish Street Hill)—and that is its proper name—is a lonely, free-standing column, extending from a point on the Thames's north bank, in the City, some 202 feet heavenwards. It is believed to have been originally designed by scientist Robert Hooke, but Sir Christopher Wren was involved in its construction. It went up in 1671 and its function is to commemorate the horrendous Great Fire of 1666, which destroyed much of the City, including the old St. Paul's Cathedral and many medieval churches, some half a hundred of which were replaced by Wren structures. If you have the strength, or the youth, or both, you may, for a small sum, ascend to the summit. There are 311 steps.

Old Bailey (on the street named for it, in the City, near St. Paul's Cathedral) is not, alas, very old. The building itself, that is. It is mostly turn-of-century with a dome apparently intended to complement that of neighboring St. Paul's. The business at hand is the trial of criminal cases in this most celebrated of the world's criminal courts. Visitors are welcome, usually mornings and afternoons, Monday through Friday. Every so often, the officers of the court toss dried flowers on the floor—a symbolic carryover from the time when the court was connected with the infamous (and smelly) Newgate Jail, which stood on the present court's site.

The Royal Exchange (Cornhill) is no longer an exchange but rather the home of an insurance company. It's the third such structure on the site and is mid-nineteenth century, with a Corinthian portico (from which new sovereigns are traditionally proclaimed) and inner quadrangle which used to be where exchange business was transacted, but which is now the site of exhibitions. The exchange's bells toll familiar tunes several times daily. The exhange is in the heart of the City's "Bank" quarter, with the Bank of England and Mansion House near-neighbors.

The St. James's Palace complex: Sovereigns have not lived in *St. James's Palace* for well over a century, but tradition dies hard in Britain and foreign ambassadors to the Crown are still accredited to the Court of St. James's. The front facade, looking out onto St. James's Street and the men's clubs that line it, is the old Tudor-era gatehouse of the palace, and the oldest part of it remaining, although there are newer sections which had been inhabited relatively recently by the late Duke of Windsor, when Prince of Wales, and his brother, the Duke of Gloucester. The remaining section of the palace include "grace and favor" apartments awarded by the Crown to the families of loyal servants, and the Chapel Royal (see Ecclesiastical London, this chapter). The palace is not open to the public, but its courtyard is, and makes for a rewarding stroll. The setting is, after all, the onetime home of Henry VIII and his children, Edward VI, Bloody Mary and Elizabeth I, not to mention other sovereigns through to William IV and Queen Adelaide. Ever since, oaths of office have been administered to monarchs at St. James's—right through to Elizabeth II, in 1952—and it is from the palace balcony that, on the death of the sovereign, the traditional proclamation is made: "The King is dead! Long live the King!"

Marlborough House is named for no less a personage than the first Duke of Marlborough, although it was the pet project of his Duchess, Sarah, who commissioned Sir Christopher Wren to design it as the couple's town house, while Sir James Vanbrugh with whom the tempestuous Sarah had fallen out—was putting up the Blenheim Palace she came to despise. She fell out with Sir Christopher, too, before Marlborough was completed. But not too late for his felicitous designs for the place to have taken shape by the builders. Sarah, who outlived her onetime intimate friend Queen Anne, as well as her husband, died an old, ever-irascible lady, at Marlborough House in 1744; Marlboroughs stayed on there until George IV's time, when the Royal Family took title. After William IV died, his widow, Dowager Queen Adelaide, moved in upon the accession of her niece, Victoria, to the throne.

Later, Marlborough House was home to Victoria's eldest son, while he was Prince of Wales (he had to add a story for his large family). When the Prince of Wales became Edward VII and moved up the Mall to Buckingham Palace, his younger son, the Duke of York—later George V—moved in. When George acceded, his widowed mother, Queen Alexandra, succeeded him at Marlborough House, and upon the death of George V in 1936, George's widow, Queen Mary, returned to the house she had known as the Duchess of York, remaining there—the place furnished with the fine antiques she had collected, but still with no modern plumbing—until she died in 1953. A few years later, Queen Mary's granddaughter, Elizabeth II, signed a Royal Warrant turning the house over to the British Government, so that it could be converted into a house for the use of Commonwealth prime ministers when in London for their conferences, and organizations having to do with Commonwealth matters.

Consequently, the house bears little resemblance to its early Wren period, or even to more recent royal occupancies. Still, the plasterwork, fireplaces and ceilings of the principal main-floor rooms are pretty much intact, and so are the paintings depicting the Duke of Marlborough's battles, in the main hall (Battle of Blenheim), the main staircase (Battle of Ramillies) and the east staircase (Battle of Malplaquet). Upstairs would be unrecognizable to anyone who knew it during Mary's day, or before. All of the rooms save an Edwardian smoking room have been turned into workaday offices. Queen Mary's beautiful sitting room—the historic one in which her son Edward VIII revealed to his mother and sister his plans to abdicate, as portrayed in the hit play, *Crown Matrimonial*—is now, rather sadly, an impersonal steel-and-leatherette conference room.

Lancaster House, much newer than Marlborough, went up in

1825 as a town house for the then Duke of York, whose name was given to it. In 1827, after the Duke's premature death, it became the property of the Marquess of Stafford, who gave it his name and enlarged it, adding to it, among other things, a Staircase Hall that remains the knock-'em-dead Staircase Hall of all time. It is as high as the house itself, is the work of Sir Charles Barry, and is illuminated from above by an absolutely enormous lantern. Corinthian columns support the elaborate ceiling from the second-floor level, and the walls are surfaced ingeniously in _faux-marbre_ inset with a series of Italian copies of Veronese paintings.

The rest of the house is anticlimactic after the Staircase Hall, with the exception of the gold-and-ivory Great Gallery upstairs. Lancaster House, since 1912, has been the property of the British Government (as distinct from the British Crown)—a gift from Viscount Leverhulme, its last private owner. The government uses it for luncheons and for receptions—and to hold conferences. (You've read about them on the Court page of _The Times_ and _The Daily Telegraph._) The fanciest post-World War II event was Prime Minister Sir Winston Churchill's luncheon in the Great Gallery honoring Queen Elizabeth II on her Coronation.

Clarence House, just beyond St. James's, is the same age as Lancaster House and is named for its first resident, King William IV, who was Duke of Clarence at the time. It has been a royal residence ever since. The current occupant is Queen Elizabeth the Queen Mother, who replaced her daughter Queen Elizabeth II, and her son-in-law, the Duke of Edinburgh, as residents when they succeeded her at Buckingham Palace, after the death of King George VI. Not open to the public.

Scotland Yard (Broadway): Alas, Inspector Alleyn fans, the "New," which became a part of Scotland Yard's title when it moved in 1890 from Whitehall, has never been more apt. Scotland Yard, or more accurately the Metropolitan Police, moved from its atmospheric Victorian building on the Victoria Embankment, to _really_ new quarters—an entire building at that—on Broadway, off Victoria Street, in 1967. (You can't go in unless, perhaps, your name is Ngaio Marsh.) To a passer-by, the new Yard looks like an ordinary glass and concrete office tower. But I am told that within are the very latest in laboratories, TV and radio communications, and the noted Criminal Records Office.

The Stock Exchange (Old Broad Street) is, along with the neighboring Bank of England, the financial core of the Commonwealth. Security market buffs will enjoy the view from the balcony of the trading sessions on the floor, Monday through Fridays, usually from 10 A.M. to 3:15 P.M.

University of London (Bloomsbury): Overshadowed by Oxford and Cambridge, both of which are centuries older, the relatively modern (1836) University of London is bound to be underestimated. It has 36,000 students in thirty-five colleges and fourteen specialized institutes, and its principal buildings are in Bloomsbury, near the British Museum. Built with a Rockefeller Foundation grant in the nineteen-twenties, they were dedicated by George V in 1933, and include the 210-foot-high Tower, a Library of 900,000 volumes, and the Senate House, for administration. There are two first-rank museums, of which more later under Museums: the Courtauld Institute and the Percival David Foundation of Chinese Art. University College, older than the University of London, of which it is now a part, goes back to 1828 and has its own home on Gower Street. It has some 5,000 students in a number of faculties, including the Slade School of Art. Also on Gower Street are the globally-renowned London School of Tropical Medicine and Royal Academy of Dramatic Art.

ECCLESIASTICAL LONDON: AFTER THE ABBEY AND ST. PAUL'S

Next to Rome, London is Europe's greatest church city, surpassing Paris and, indeed, all of the other European capitals. Norman (the British way of saying Romanesque), Gothic, Renaissance, Baroque, even a cathedral in Byzantine style: London has them all. The pity is that, given its wealth of other diversions, many visitors stop after the earlier-described Westminster Abbey and St. Paul's Cathedral. What follows is a representative sampling of churches that I like, beginning with a dozen special standouts, followed by a quartet designed by the prolific James Gibbs, ten from among the half-hundred by Sir Christopher Wren (most of whose churches are in the City), with half a dozen additional non-Wren City churches. Appended is still another group, to illustrate the diversity of the religious scene in London, and to suggest places of worship for visitors of various faiths.

A Dozen-plus All-London Standouts:

Southwark Cathedral does not attempt to compete with Westminster Abbey, although perhaps it should. Across the river, in South London, as its name connotes, it is, after the Abbey, the greatest Gothic church in London. Southwark was antedated by an earlier Norman church, but its more or less present Gothic look dates from the twelfth through the fifteenth centuries, when the elaborate choir and the fine transepts were constructed. The high nave, though in a Gothic style consistent with the rest of the church, is actually Victorian. Although Southwark has been a cathedral or, in other words, the seat of a bishop in charge of a diocese, only since the turn of the present century, it is not without a rich history. During the unhappy reign of Henry VIII's elder daughter, the Catholic Bloody Mary, Protestant martyrs were tried in Southwark. James VI was married there. And John Harvard, founder of the American university bearing his name, was baptized there (the Harvard Chapel of the Cathedral honors him). Walk over, if you're in the City, via either Southwark or London Bridge. There are special events at lunchtime—musical or otherwise—on weekdays, in addition to regular services.

Westminster Cathedral: There are some six million Roman Catholics in Britain, and enough of them live in and around London for it to constitute an archdiocese headed by an archbishop of cardinal's rank, whose seat is the turn-of-the-century Westminster Cathedral. This is London's least-known major church, and more's the pity. Its style is Byzantine, which architect John Francis Bentley wisely selected over the prevalent neo-Gothic of the time because it would enable more rapid completion, greater space and—most important—it would be much cheaper. Although the cathedral opened in 1903, it still—not unlike the also-immense Cathedral of St. John the Divine in New York—is not completed. Only half of the dozen chapels which ring the nave are decorated with the mosaics intended for them. Because it is so relatively unknown, I cite a few statistics. The length is 360 feet. The nave is 117 feet high, and the campanile—or bell tower (to which, please note, there is an elevator to take visitors to an observation tower that affords a smashing view of London)—is 273 feet high. Within, the nave is England's widest, with a capacity of 2,000, all seated and able to see the sumptuous high altar, over which suspended from the ceiling, is an immense red and gold cross. Of the half-dozen completed chapels, the loveliest are Blessed Sacrament, St. Paul's and Holy Souls. The cathedral has what must be the longest open-hours of any London destination—6 A.M. to 9 P.M. every day. Underground: Victoria Station.

St. Margaret's, Westminster (Parliament Square) is, because it is part of the Westminster Abbey complex, overshadowed by the Abbey, at least by many casual visitors. Londoners are more familiar with it, for it has been the official church of the House of Commons for some four of its ten centuries, and perhaps even more significant to readers of society pages, it is the venue for fashionable weddings. St. Margaret's bridegrooms have included Samuel Pepys, John Milton and Sir Winston Churchill. It has had considerable alteration over the centuries, the most important a sixteenth-century rebuilding in the perpendicular Gothic style. Very beautiful.

Brompton Oratory (Brompton Road) is, like Westminster Cathedral, Roman Catholic, and is, again like Westminster Cathedral, of a refreshingly uncommon-to-London style. You have the not unpleasant feeling, with the oratory, that you're in Rome or Florence. It is a late nineteenth-century variation of Italian Renaissance, and you might want to visit it in connection with one of the musical programs for which it is noted. At any rate, it's a neighbor of the Victoria and Albert Museum worth bearing in mind when you visit the V and A.

The Chapel Royal of St. James's Palace is the only part of the palace (the courtyard going through it excepted) that is open to the public, and then only for Sunday services, usually in winter. It is a mostly Gothic structure, with its chef d'oeuvre the splendid ceiling which Holbein is believed to have painted, and with easily discernible royal initials—"H" for Henry VIII, the monarch whom Holbein immortalized on canvas, and "A," believed to stand for Anne of Cleves, Wife No. 4, to whom Henry was married in 1540, the date appearing on the ceiling. Other queens were married in the chapel, too, not least among them being Victoria, just three centuries to the year after Anne and Henry.

The Queen's Chapel (Marlborough House) is just a hop and a skip from the Chapel Royal (above), and is a lovely Inigo Jones work named for Queen Henrietta Maria, the wife of Charles I, who inaugurated it. Try taking in a service, for the choir boys' gowns are as they have been for centuries and the royal pews are unchanged since Henrietta Maria and Charles were their first occupants.

The Chapel Royal of St. Peter ad Vincula, in the Tower of London, is the oldest of England's chapels royal, dating to the twelfth century, and where many sovereigns worshiped, including two— Queen Anne Boleyn and Queen Katherine Parr—just before they were executed. The Gothic look of the place remains. The choir's musical skills are esteemed; visitors are welcome at the two Sunday morning services, and do not have to pay the usual Tower admission fee to participate in them.

The Chelsea Royal Hospital Chapel, like the hospital itself, was designed by Wren, with its chief decorative element a massive mural called, "The Last Muster." A Sunday service—with the pensioners in their traditional uniform, the choir in equally old-style vestments—is a special treat.

The Guards' Chapel, Wellington Barracks (Birdcage Walk), is essentially post-World War II, for the beautiful old chapel was badly bombed. Some of the old remains, though, and there is always music by one of the various Guards' regiment bands at the Sunday services to which visitors are welcome.

The Temple Church (Temple) is the place of worship shared by the Inner Temple and the Middle Temple, two of the four London Inns of Court. It goes back some eight hundred years, combining Gothic and Romanesque features impressively, with a chancel of the former period appended to the original round church of the latter. One of London's most impressive smaller places of worship.

All Souls' (Langham Place at Regent Street) is special in that it was designed by John Nash, the great Regency architect. It was war-damaged but the restoration is commendable, and the interior is quite as lovely as the near-circular exterior is distinctive.

St. Peter's (Eaton Square) is one to have a look at when you are inspecting Belgravia. A landmark of rectangular Eaton Square, it is a late nineteenth-century neoclassic structure, understandably popular for *haute monde* weddings.

St. Mary Abbots (Kensington High Street), is an oasis of quiet and beauty in the heart of Kensington, just opposite Barkers department store. It is Victorian neo-Gothic (1872) in the very best sense of that term, with an unusually tall spire (278 feet) and among other attributes an unusual cloistered walkway. Pop in for a rest, while doing the Kensington shops.

A Quartet by James Gibbs:

James Gibbs's output in the first half of the eighteenth century embraced ten London churches, not to mention important work at both Cambridge and Oxford. He was later than Wren and was obviously influenced by that master, with the result handsomely and typically Georgian. Gibbs's work in turn (particularly St. Martin-in-the-Fields) inspired countless designers of the steepled churches which became a commonplace of colonial America.

St. Martin-in-the-Fields (Trafalgar Square) was completed by Gibbs in 1726, and George I, the first of the Hanoverian sovereigns, was its first churchwarden. His coat of arms remains in the church above the chancel arch. To this day St. Martin's is the sovereign's parish church, Buckingham Palace falling within its boundaries. It is, as well, the official church of the Admiralty, the ministry that has jurisdiction over the Royal Navy. (There are both Royal and Admiralty pews.) There is a sumptuous gilded and cream ceiling, supported by rows of Corinthian columns, their capitals gilded like the ceiling. The pulpit has Grinling Gibbons carving. The National Gallery and National Portrait Gallery are near neighbors, and a St. Martin's inspection is well combined with a visit to them.

Grosvenor Chapel (South Audley Street) is a charming Gibbs church, just off Grosvenor Square, the site of the American Embassy and for that reason a gathering place for many Americans, both military and otherwise, during World War II. U.S. troops worshiped frequently at the church during the war, and there is a plaque within, recording the special American association with the Grosvenor parish.

St. Mary-le-Strand (Strand) is, rather ingeniously, built upon a tiny island in one of London's most horrendously traffic-filled thoroughfares, so that by the time you are able to cross the street to gain admittance, you feel constrained to offer thanks in the church for having arrived safely, at the same time praying that you will be able to make an equally safe exit from the little island to the across-the-street sidewalk. Still, the trip is worth the effort. There is a pretty little flower garden, carefully fenced off from the entrance steps, and within, an exquisite gilded ceiling shelters a neoclassic interior. En route out, before you step into that traffic, look up at the handsome white steeple.

St. Peter's (Vere Street) is another small Gibbs treasure, just off Cavendish Square, north of Wigmore Street, and still substantially Georgian. St. Peter's, completed in 1724, antedated St. Martin-in-the-Fields, and is a kind of St. Martin in miniature.

Ten by Wren:

Aside from the earlier-described St. Paul's, Sir Christopher Wren designed more than fifty London churches, most in the City. By no means all have survived World War II intact; of some, only towers or less remain. Others have been beautifully restored. What follow are ten Wren churches that I especially like. The first, a non-City church, is located in tourist-trod Piccadilly.

St. James's (Piccadilly) is one of Wren's larger churches. It was completed in 1684. Its devastation during World War II was almost complete, except for not much more than its four walls and the base of its steeple. The restoration, with the exception of an unfortunate Victorian-type stained glass window behind the altar, has been first rate, with the glorious arched ceiling as it was, and the baroque organ rebuilt (Grinling Gibbons carved the gilded cherubs atop it).

St. Bride's (Fleet Street) stands on a site that has known churches of one sort or other for some sixteen centuries. It is a restoration of a brilliant Wren church that was the eighth on the site, and below which has been found the remains of a Roman house. St. Bride's has considerable literary and journalistic associations. Its worshipers have included Chaucer, Shakespeare, Milton, Evelyn and Pepys. The Wren church which replaced the edifice destroyed in the Great Fire, opened in 1675. World War II saw devastation again. The restoration, though, was unsurpassed in London churches, and includes the creation of a new, Wren-style reredos, or altar frame, as a result of which the sanctuary looks even more handsome than it did before the war. Queen Elizabeth II rededicated the rebuilt church in 1957; it was made possible by contributions from Fleet Street newspaper-world neighbors. But the American press has a soft spot for St. Bride's, too. Among the memorial plaques is one given to honor U.S. journalists who lost their lives in the course of their work abroad, by the Overseas Press Club of America, largely through the efforts of an old colleague and friend of mine, the late Madeline Dane

Ross, who visited St. Bride's on frequent London visits and had been stationed in Europe during World War II.

St. Clement Danes (Strand) is, like the earlier-described St. Mary-le-Strand, on an island in the Strand. It is much less harrowing to reach, however, and it is much larger and more ambitious. Indeed, it is one of Wren's grandest churches. Like most of its sister City churches, it was terribly damaged during World War II. But the restoration was brilliant, and in the process the Royal Air Force adopted the church as its official place of worship; countless bronze RAF squadron insignia are embedded in the church floor, and the names of World War II dead appear in a memorial register. This is the church of "Oranges and Lemons say the bells of St. Clements" and the nursery rhyme is commemorated annually at a youngsters' service at which each child receives an orange and a lemon. Withal, the interior of the church, architecturally, is what makes it most stand out—pulpit, painted reredos, U. S. Air Force-donated organ, and the magnificent ceiling supported by graceful Corinthian columns.

St. James Garlickhythe (Upper Thames Street) seems dwarfed by its substantial steeple and is a great surprise within, for its ceiling is the highest of any in the City. The decor is severely—and elegantly—simple and of surpassing beauty. Hythe, I learned from the verger, used to mean cove—a place where ships tied up and, in this instance, one assumes, where their chief cargo was garlic.

St. Lawrence Jewry (Gresham Street) is extra-substantial Wren, in keeping with its designation as the official church of the Corporation, or Council, of the City of London. Its lengthy rectangular interior is accented by a series of handsome brass chandeliers, splendid plasterwork, and typical dark-wood pews, altar and organ. Guildhall is next door.

St. Mary Abchurch (Abchurch Lane off Cannon Street) is distinguished by a stunning painted dome that dominates the whole of the lovely squarish interior, contrast coming from white walls and the dark wood of the superb Grinling Gibbons-carved altar. A knockout.

St. Benet, Paul's Wharf (Upper Thames Street), has an exceptionally graceful exterior with garlands of stone atop each of the fine, clear-paned windows. Within, the feeling is one of great height. The ceiling plasterwork is exceptional. If you don't understand the language being spoken, fear not: services in Welsh are conducted here.

St. Mary-le-Bow (Cheapside) is oddly Italianate Wren—light walls and ceilings are of a piece. A great gold crucifix hangs from the ceiling in the center of the church. The floors are black-and-white marble. The feeling is of tremendous, luxuriant space. There is a Norman crypt below and a super steeple.

St. Mary Aldermary (Watling Street) is a Wren shocker: the master in a Gothic mood, and it works, if one overlooks a bit of well-meant Victorian gussying-up around the altar. Wren's ceiling is his version of Gothic fan vaulting, and a beauty. There are side aisles framed by Gothic arches, and the other Wren-Gothic touches are charming too.

St. Stephen Walbrook (Walbrook) is another Italianate Wren, with a series of sixteen columns lining the inside of the oblong interior, and framing an immense coffered dome. Oddly, somewhat heavily handsome—but with style.

Additional Mostly Anglican Churches:

St. Etheldreda's (Ely Place) is the first pre-Reformation church to be returned from Anglican to Roman Catholic jurisdiction and stands in a little-visited City cul-de-sac named for a no-longer-standing Bishop's palace. Until the Catholics bought the church in 1875 and restored its original name, it had been known since the Reformation as Ely Chapel, after the house to which it had been attached. It is a Gothic treasure, well restored after World War II. The west window, originally fourteenth century, is said

to be one of the biggest in all London. There is a little cloister
and a crypt, as well.

St. Bartholomew the Great (West Smithfield) is essentially a
Romanesque (Norman, as the British say) church that is, except
for St. John the Evangelist Chapel in the Tower of London, the
oldest in town. It is a neighbor both of St. Bartholomew's Hospital
(the oldest in London) and the smaller (and partially newer)
St. Bartholomew the Less Church. St. Bartholomew the Great
goes back to the early twelfth century, and although much of it
was destroyed at the time of the Reformation, enough remains—
the masterful choir, part of the nave, other architectural treasures—to make the church one of the first rank.

St. Olave, Hart Street (off Fenchurch Street), is a beautiful
Gothic church entered through its own wall-enclosed yard (the
benches are nice for a rest on a busy sight-seeing day). The building is essentially fifteenth century—with stone walls, Gothic-
arched windows and aisles, and a fine beamed ceiling. Mr. and
Mrs. Samuel Pepys were members of the Parish (there is a bust
of Mrs. Pepys erected by her husband) and the church conducts
an annual Pepys Week.

St. Helen's, Bishopsgate (Bishopsgate) is another basically Gothic
church. It is more elaborate than St. Olave, with Renaissance
pieces, and additions of other eras, even including a Victorian
screen. The flattish timbered roof evokes medieval times; so,
for that matter, does the church as a whole, its more modern
appurtenances notwithstanding.

St. Dunstan-in-the-West (Fleet Street) is early nineteenth-century neo-Gothic, with a winning octagonal shape, a wedding-cake
tower, and an interior more comfortable and inviting than distinguished. Agreeable for a pause after, say, Dr. Johnson's House,
in nearby Gough Square.

St. Botolph Without Aldgate (Aldgate High Street). Botolph, the
patron saint of English travelers, a kind of U.K. St. Christopher,

was English-born himself (seventh century) and so popular that in the City alone there are three churches named for him, two with locations so similar-sounding that they can be confusing. (One is at Bishopsgate but the other two are at Aldersgate and Aldgate.) All three are of interest, but I have selected Aldgate. It is mostly mid-eighteenth century, high-ceilinged with Doric columns for support, and plasterwork not necessarily the most graceful in town. There is an interesting social and ecumenical thrust. Members of the parish have an open house nightly in the crypt for London's equivalent of Bowery bums, and there are effective programs, too, with young people and with the church's Jewish neighbors.

Other London Places of Worship:

Bloomsbury Central Baptist Church, Shaftesbury Avenue; *First Church of Christ Scientist,* Sloane Terrace; *Westminster Congregational Chapel,* Buckingham Gate, Westminster; *West London Synagogue* (Reform), Upper Berkeley Street; *Central Synagogue* (Orthodox), Great Portland Street; *St. Anne and St. Agnes Lutheran Church* (seventeenth century), Gresham Street; *John Wesley's Chapel* (Methodist, built 1778), City Road; *Regent Square Presbyterian Church,* Regent Square; *St. Sophia* (Greek Orthodox) *Cathedral,* Moscow Road; *Westminster Friends Meeting House,* 52 St. Martin's Lane; *Salvation Army Regent Hall,* 2750 Oxford Street; *The Spiritualist Association,* 33 Belgrave Square; *Hindu Center,* 39 Grafton Terrace; *Central Mosque,* 146 Park Road; *Sikh Temple,* 79 Sinclair Road; *Buddhist Society,* 58 Eccleston Square.

MUSEUMGOER'S LONDON: A SELECTED SCORE-AND-FOUR

Along with New York, Paris and Rome, London is one of the pre-eminent museum cities. Its museums reflect not only the richness and diversity of Britain's own culture but the cultures—as manifested through art and artifacts—of diverse peoples of other areas of the world, many of whom the British came to know

during the days of the Empire. The British Museum, earlier described, perhaps more than any other, reflects the acquisitions
made available to a major imperial power. It, and the National
Portrait Gallery—the latter because it sets the stage for London—
are among the Top Ten London attractions in this book. But they
are only a starter, for museums. I have selected an additional score
of museums that I especially like. Here they are:

The National Gallery is the splendid neoclassic building that
dominates Trafalgar Square. It is so conveniently located that I
marvel more of my countrymen don't go in. It houses one of
the superlative collections of old masters, but it is strong, as well,
on the French Impressionists. The range, in other words, is
European painting from the thirteenth century through the nineteenth, both British and Continental. There are more than a score
of galleries on the main floor, with a dreary restaurant-café in
the basement and a first-rate shop, with an enormous selection of
postcards, catalogues and art books, at the main entrance.

But it is the pictures that make the gallery. The Italian medieval work—Masolino's Saints John the Baptist and Jerome, for
example—is a joy. One sees as well Bronzino and Titian, Bellini
and Botticelli among the Italians, who are possibly no better represented anywhere else outside of Italy; Vermeer and Rembrandt (represented by a whopping nineteen paintings) among
the Dutch; Goya, Murillo and Velasquez among the Spaniards.
The Golden English eighteenth century of Reynolds, Gainsborough, Hogarth and their contemporaries, is strongly represented, along with later British greats like Constable and Turner.
The eighteenth-century French—Watteau and Chardin—are present, and there are many galleries of later French work—Degas,
Manet, Cézanne, Seurat, Monet, Renoir. Ideally, a minimum
of two fairly long half-day visits is recommended. Then you find
yourself popping in, on return trips, whenever you pass by.

The Tate Gallery (Millbank) is outstanding for its specialties,
British painting from the Renaissance onward, and modern work
from the Impressionists through to, say, last week. In the superlative English section there are fine Hogarths, Gainsboroughs and

Reynoldses. But the star of the Tate is J. M. W. Turner, the early-nineteenth-century English painter who was a good half century ahead of his time and who is better represented at this museum than at any other.

There are exceptionally strong Constable and Blake sections, too, and some fine French Impressionists and post-Impressionists. The museum building is attractive and a joy to explore, with a good shop for postcards, greeting cards and the Tate's own series of art books, and—an unusual treat for London—an attractive restaurant that happily lacks the gloom of most of its museum-restaurant counterparts.

Victoria and Albert Museum (Cromwell Road, South Kensington)—the "V and A" to Londoners—is a unit of the group of South Kensington museums (the others are the Science, Natural History and Geological museums) devised by Queen Victoria's German consort, Prince Albert, after his hugely successful Great Exhibition of 1851. Victoria herself laid the cornerstone in 1899, not long before she died; her son, Edward VII, opened the building in 1909—not long before he died. The V and A is a great repository of the decorative arts. Not only British. And not only decorative. The fine arts are well represented, too. The emphasis is on European work from the Middle Ages onward. Not unexpectedly, English furniture and furnishings are particularly strong. But there are treasures ranging from paintings by Raphael to Renaissance ship models of solid gold. The special shows are invariably imaginative.

All this said, let me add that on first visit the immense, cavernous, high-ceilinged museum can be intimidating and overwhelming. In no London museum, save the British, is one better advised to first buy the official guidebook—inexpensive and excellent—or the even cheaper map of the galleries. In order to make a tour meaningful, the authorities have devised a group of fifteen "primary" galleries, in which the very best exhibits are gathered by category. These are supplemented with the remainder of the collection in other galleries known as the Departmental (or Study) Collections.

In all events, the not-to-be-missed exhibits are the room settings

—a room from Clifford's Inn, London, of the late seventeenth century; a room from Henrietta Place, London, designed by James Gibbs (the earlier-described church architect of St. Martin-in-the-Fields and many other structures); a room from a house in Hatton Garden, London, of the early eighteenth century; the music room from Norfolk House, London (mid-eighteenth century), a Gothic Revival room out of Kent, late eighteenth century and the work of James Wyatt; another chamber by the earlier-described Robert Adam, not to mention a Regency room of Thomas Hope, a leading designer of that period, and other settings illustrating the contribution of designers ranging from the exuberant William Kent to the severely simple William Morris; with exhibits continuing through the decoratively uninhibited Victorians to such forerunners of our own era's contemporary design as Charles Rennie Mackintosh and C. R. Ashbee.

The shops for V and A postcards as well as the museum's own excellent series of books on the decorative art are a pleasure. There are, as well, a big, albeit unexciting cafeteria, as well as a drab waitress-service tearoom where equally drab set-teas are served. One wishes the V and A would put its expertise at the decorative arts to work in these two eateries.

The Courtauld Institute Galleries (Woburn Square) is one of London's—and all Europe's—best-kept museum surprises. A unit of the University of London and with a Bloomsbury location near the British Museum, the Courtauld—one floor up in a nondescript building via an enormous and rather creaky self-service elevator—is an absolute treasure. There are two major collections. The best known is of Impressionists and post-Impressionists—the collection of the late Samuel Courtauld, an industrialist. Manet's "A Bar at the Folies-Bergère" in itself makes a visit worthwhile. But consider also Toulouse-Lautrec's "La Chambre Separée," Monet's "Vase de Fleurs," Renoir's "La Loge," and Gauguin's "Haymaking."

There is, as well, a collection of old masters given by Lord Lee of Fareham, with particularly rich Italian representation—Boticelli, Bellini, Veronese, Tintoretto, for example—but with other painters' work, too. I particularly like the Cranach "Adam and Eve" and a lady called Mrs. Malcolm, as painted by Sir Henry Raeburn. The guards are the only nasty ones I've encountered in London, angrily ready to pounce if they think a visitor might get too close to a painting. There is neither shop nor restaurant, merely a postcard counter operated by bored-appearing students, busy with their studies. But no bore the Courtauld; nor for that matter, the Courtauld-operated *Home House,* a Robert Adam-designed masterwork on Portman Square.

The Buckingham Palace museums (Buckingham Palace Road): British sovereigns can be excused not opening their London home to the public; none in Europe save the Swedish monarchs open the town palaces they live in to visitors. And in Britain, suburban Windsor Castle is available to inspectors-at-large, not to mention Kensington, where the Queen's sister lives, and Marlborough House, where her grandmother lived. If Buckingham proper is not open to the public, two parts of it are.

The first, and more visited of the two, is the *Queen's Gallery,* occupying part of a former chapel, and entered from Buckingham Palace Road, not the palace's front door. The space being relatively small, the exhibition policy is eminently sound. There is no permanent exhibit. Rather, the show changes once or twice a year and consists of groupings of works from Her Majesty's priceless private collections, largely of Old Masters. Not to be missed.

The other Palace museum has far more restricted open hours. It is called the *Royal Mews* and is entered by its own impressive gateway also on Buckingham Palace Road. This is Her Majesty's stables, with which are incorporated a museum of royal coaches. There are, of course, other coach museums in Europe—those of Lisbon and Munich's Nymphenburg Palace come to mind. What make the Mews unique is that the coaches, most of them at least, are still in use when the occasion demands —the Gold State Coach, for example, dates from George III's reign, and still is used at coronations. The Irish State Coach goes to work every year when the sovereign opens Parliament. The

State Landau is used regularly when Queen Elizabeth fetches visiting foreign heads of state from railway stations. There are a lot more, and there are, as well, the comfortably housed royal horses, the corps of coachmen and grooms who headquarter here, and historic photographs of monarchs or their families, atop the backs of their horses. Quite special.

The Wallace Collection (Manchester Square) occupies Hertford House, the capacious eighteenth-century dwelling of the Dukes of Manchester on a still lovely square just north of Oxford Street. It has an ambience not unlike that of New York's Frick Collection, except that Hertford House gives the impression of having been considerably more lived in than Henry Clay Frick's formal New World Palace on Manhattan's Fifth Avenue. The Wallace Collection was a gift to the British people from the widow of Sir Richard Wallace who, with his ancestors, had collected it mostly in France. The Renaissance paintings are the chief lure— the great Dutch and Flemish artists are all present. But the French are big—eighteenth century mainly. And so are the Spaniards and the English. Painting is only part of the collection; there is armor, for example, and a French eighteenth-century furniture group is a treat. A charmer.

The London Museum (The Barbican) appears even less appreciated than the Museum of the City of New York and Paris's Carnavalet—two of its counterparts. Which is a great pity, indeed, for this is a jewel of a repository of Londoniana down through the ages, in an enchanting setting—the Royal Palace of Kensington. The time span is astonishing. You start with the prehistoric era, continue through the Dark Ages, the formative period of Roman London, or Londinium, and continue on through medieval, Tudor, later-Renaissance, Georgian, Regency, Victorian-Edwardian, and contemporary London, represented— among other objects—by Queen Elizabeth II's coronation robe. There are ancient coins, precious glass, furniture (including the bed slept in by King James II and his alliteratively named Queen, Mary of Modena, during their unhappy three-year reign; and a no-nonsense Victorian fire engine. An eye opener.

Sir John Soane's Museum (13 Lincoln's Inn Fields) is where the prolific architect lived the last quarter century (1813–37) of a long and never-dull-for-a-moment life. The setting is a big, beautiful, still largely eighteenth-century City square, and the house, while eminently habitable, was designed by Sir John as both home and museum. The contents include plans of his designs, and an astonishing variety of art and antiques. He was a man of taste, not to mention formidable talent (the Bank of England—with parts of his original still remaining—was only one of his projects).

He had catholic interests and the exhibits reflect them—a catacomblike chamber with Roman relics, rare Egyptian works in the so-called Sepulchral Chamber, ancient Greek sculpture, considerable Italian art, other paintings—England's Turner as well as Venice's Canaletto, not to mention a Lawrence of Sir John himself. But the most fascinating of the exhibits are two Hogarth series—"The Election" and "The Rake's Progress." They are explained in detail by a resident guard, standing before a prominent wall sign directing visitors not to tip their lecturer. There will indeed always be an England.

The Wellington Museum (Apsley House, Hyde Park Corner) is the first Duke of Wellington's London digs and quite grand enough to be mistaken for a royal residence. Robert Adam was the original designer of the place, but the Iron Duke elaborated on the Adam work, setting Benjamin Wyatt to work, with the resulting Corinthian portico over the front entrance and a stone facing. A contemporary descendant of the original duke gave the house and its contents to the nation after World War II, and its administrator is the knowledgeable Victoria and Albert Museum, which runs a few other big houses, including Ham and Osterley Park. Apsley House is far too much of a catch-all repository of Wellingtoniana to emerge as beautifully as either Ham or Osterley. But it is hardly without interest.

To at least one visitor, the most remarkable exhibit is in the dining room—a service of silver plate from the Regent of Portugal that took well over a hundred silversmiths several years to create. The entrance hall catches one up with its larger-than-

life statue of Napoleon clad only in a fig leaf (if one excepts
the shawl draped over an extended arm). There are other
similarly eccentric treasures. But there are, as well, some superb
paintings—including one of Wellington by Sir Thomas Lawrence.
And you can't beat the location.

The Greenwich complex: Getting there is half the fun. There
are quick express trains from Charing Cross Station, rather more
complex bus routings, and the most fun of all, via the Thames,
in summer, both rapid hydrofoil and much slower conventional
boat. Greenwich first comes up in history as Placentia Palace, the
very same in which Henry VIII lived, and where his daughter,
Queen Elizabeth I, was born. Later, in the seventeenth century,
during the reign of William and Mary, Sir Christopher Wren
was commissioned by the Crown to design a naval hospital to
replace an earlier palace that had succeeded the Tudor Placentia.

Wren's hospital—since 1873 the *Royal Naval College*—surpasses St. Paul's Cathedral as his masterwork, at least to one
observer. Utilizing the position of the earlier (and still standing)
Inigo Jones-designed Queen's House—inland from the Thames
—as a focal point, he created two grand colonnades leading
to and framing in the background the Queen's House, and
doubling as walls of the pair of domed blocks that constitute
hospital-cum-college. Because the college remains very much in
business, with midshipmen inhabiting it, its two great interiors
may usually be seen only in the afternoon (unless the long-
standing hours are changed).

You are, therefore, urged to plan your Greenwich visit to include the mid-afternoon hours so that you can take in the college's
Painted Hall (with breathtaking murals on both the walls and the
high ceiling by Sir James Thornhill) that is now the midshipmen's
dining room; and the big and ever so beautiful, originally Wren
Chapel, with a splendid blue-and-gold ceiling and the striking
painting of St. Paul by Benjamin West behind the altar.

The earlier-mentioned *Queen's House* is now but one of three
principal sectors of the *National Maritime Museum,* which ranks
with the Musée de la Marine in Paris as a world leader of its

type. The museum exhibits ships models and plans, navigational instruments, naval weapons and uniforms, all manner of printed matter relating to matters maritime, paintings of exceptional caliber as to constitute a major surprise. Personal favorites: Elizabeth I by an unidentified genius; Charles I by the studio of Daniel Luytens; Queen Henrietta Maria by Van Dyck; Nelson by L. F. Abbott, and Lady Hamilton by Romney. The Queen's House itself is, after all, a former royal palace whose genius of a designer pioneered it a century ahead of his time. Other museum buildings flank the Queen's House. The East Wing is where one enters, and exhibits nineteenth and twentieth century exhibits. The West Wing, to at least one visitor, is far more interesting with its highlights the sections on Captain Cook and his exploits, and Nelson and his battles. The Queen's House, appropriately enough, is for the earlier centuries through the Renaissance, with fine paintings, a fantastic circular staircase, and sumptuous chambers, including the East Bridge Room and the bedroom inhabited by the queen for whom the house was named—Henrietta Maria, wife of Charles I.

There are other Greenwich attractions: Wren-designed Flamstead, the original *Royal Observatory* building, outside which is the Greenwich Meridian-Longitude Zero, marked across the observatory's courtyard. Nearby is the venerable sailing vessel, *Cutty Sark* (the whiskey was named for it, not vice versa). In Greenwich is a charmer of a church, *St. Alfege,* the work of Wren's assistant, Nicholas Hawksmoor, built during the reign of Queen Anne, who insisted that the church contain a royal pew—still to be observed. Make a day of it, lunching at the Trafalgar Tavern whose special lures are mementoes of Lord Nelson.

The Royal Academy of Arts (Burlington House, Piccadilly) is housed in the palatial, albeit rather gloomy, mid-nineteenth century, neo-Renaissance pile that has become a Piccadilly landmark. The academy, a century older than its present home, has been having annual summer shows for more than two centuries; the exhibitors are British, selected by means of fierce competition, and the dates are usually May through July or August. There are, as well, occasional special—and not necessarily

British—exhibits, which can be of high caliber. The academy's membership is exclusive and selected through a complicated process; Sir Christopher Wren was an early president. There is nothing royal about the restaurant.

Percival David Foundation of Chinese Art (53 Gordon Square) is a unit of the University of London less celebrated than its sister-museum, the Courtauld Institute Galleries, which itself is not known nearly as widely as it deserves to be. Located in a Bloomsbury town house in the sprawling University of London quarter, this is a superlative display of Chinese treasures—porcelain, enamelware, scrolls—a gift of its collector, Sir Percival David, after World War II. All told, there are some 1,500 objects surveying Chinese art for the last millennium. Nice in tandem with the Courtauld, its near neighbor.

British Theatre Museum (12 Holland Park Road) occupies fine old Leighton House with its unlikely-for-London interiors including a fountain-centered Arabian parlor. At times one has the feeling that the late Lord Leighton's other objects fight with the Museum exhibits which are presumably the house's contemporary *raison d'être*. But no matter: drama buffs, in this most theater-rich of capitals, will find Siddons' Sheraton dressing table and letters, manuscripts, photos and costumes galore—even one of Nijinsky's.

Dulwich College Picture Gallery (College Road) is a hike from central London, make no mistake. Give yourself half a day and try to select a sunny one so that you can enjoy a stroll through this unlikely South London suburb with a still bucolic air to its park-and-garden setting, and its gem: the Sir John Soane-designed (1814) picture gallery—the first public one in London. On display are a surprisingly rich collection of Old Masters—including Rembrandt and Rubens, and some fine English works as well—Lelys, Knellers, Hogarths, Ramsays, Gainsboroughs among them. The gallery is a part of the venerable institution variously known as Dulwich College and Alleyn's School, whose origins go back several centuries to founder Edward Alleyn, who may well have been the inspiration for Ngaio Marsh's fictional Scotland Yard superintendent, the well-born Roderick Alleyn; at any rate, I like to think so. Dulwich Village is still substantially Georgian in its architecture, while the college—actually a good-sized public school—is housed in a mid-Victorian building, despite its much older origins.

Foundling Hospital Art Gallery (40 Brunswick Square) is a peculiar London institution of advanced age that would be better known, no doubt, if it were open more than parts of two days each week—which has long been the case. No matter. The locale is a fine replica of the so-called Court Room; it dates back to the early eighteenth century when Hogarth encouraged fellow artists to contribute their work to the hospital. The results of Hogarth's efforts are still to be seen—work of his own, of course, plus paintings by Reynolds, West, Ramsay, and others as well as the keyboard of Handel's organ, the composer having been the volunteer leader of the hospital's choir.

Imperial War Museum (Lambeth Road). The empire is, of course, no more, but the Imperial War Museum stubbornly retains the name it has had since World War I days. You may or may not be attracted because of its associations with an empire that is no more or because the theme is war or because the setting is the original mental hospital called by a name that has become a part of the language: Bedlam. Still, the place may surprise you. What it sets out to do is show how the empire, oops, the Commonwealth, co-operated during the course of the two World Wars. The domed building, to start, is Regency and with a graceful portico. The galleries—navy, air, army—are chock full of war objects, ranging from an actual German submarine to a French tank and a World War II spitfire aircraft. The big surprise is the Picture Gallery; all of the works have war-related themes and their creators include Sargent, Wyndham Lewis, Feliks Topolski and Epstein.

Kenwood (Hampstead Heath) is visitable as a great Robert Adam house (later described) and as a museum of priceless paintings, these of the collection of brewer Edward Cecil Guinness, first Earl of Iveagh, who bequeathed them, with the house, to the public, in 1927. Kenwood, operated by the Greater London Council, constitutes a choice collection—both Gainsborough and Reynolds are heavily represented. So are Turner and Landseer, and so are the French, through Boucher and Watteau; and the Dutch, with Rembrandt and Vermeer. There is no better excuse for a sampling of the bucolic beauty of Hampstead Heath and adjoining Hampstead village.

Commonwealth Institute (Kensington High Street at Holland Park). A post-World War II structure that looks as though it might have been displaced from a world's fair, the institute is only partially a museum. It's a commendable catch-all organization designed to put the various Commonwealth countries' best feet forward to the people of the United Kingdom. Its museum aspect embraces two vast floors of exhibits—again World's Fair-like in concept—of each and every one of the Commonwealth countries. (Nigeria, in my view, is the don't-miss of the lot.) Noteworthy, too, is an art gallery with frequently changing shows of Commonwealth artists, often two or three at a time. (At one recent show there were works by a Nigerian, a New Zealander and a Briton.) There is a theater for dramatic and musical events with Commonwealth origins, and a library with the Commonwealth its subject matter. A painless enough way to get an idea of what the Commonwealth is all about. The cafeteria is plain and cheap, and there is an interesting shop with Commonwealth-made wares and books about the subject at hand.

Madame Tussaud's (Marylebone Road). I am dignifying this establishment by including it in this section of selected museums only because you will have heard of it, and you may want to go. Well, unless you see them, you can't believe how awful many of the wax statues are, particularly those of the contemporary personalities whose faces we are familiar with from newspapers, films and television. Those of most members of the current Royal Family are nothing less than embarrassing.

Memorial Houses:

Not a few writers and artists of note were native Londoners; the houses of some are contemporarily maintained as museums. Five of the most interesting follow.

Thomas Carlyle's House (24 Cheyne Row, Chelsea) is a small house on a street of small houses, and is as good an excuse as any to visit this good-looking Chelsea quarter—bordering the Thames and with more substantial Cheyne (pronounced *cheyney*) Walk its most noted thoroughfare. The house was more than a century old when Carlyle and his wife moved in, in 1834, remaining until the author died in 1881—nearly half a century. The furnishings are the Carlyles' own (the National Trust runs the house, and very well). To be seen are the top floor studio and living and bedroom, and the basement kitchen. Written under this roof were such works as *The French Revolution* and *Frederick the Great.*

Charles Dickens' House (48 Doughty Street) was Dickens' home for only two years (1837–39) but the prolific author, in that brief period, wrote *Oliver Twist* and *Nicholas Nicholby* there and worked on parts of a couple of other books as well. A highlight of the house, especially for Dickens buffs, is a remarkably complete library of and about Dickens, as well as a Pickwick-type kitchen belowstairs, and a host of Dickensiana. It's all under the aegis of the worthy organization called the Dickens Fellowship.

William Hogarth's House (Hogarth Lane, Chiswick) pales in contrast to its considerably more opulent neighbor, the Palladian Chiswick House (see page 68). Still, considering that it was badly damaged during World War II, and has had to be restored, it conveys a picture of what it must have been when Hogarth and his wife used it as a country retreat in the mid-eighteenth century, as a respite from their town house. There is precious little furniture, more's the pity, but there are considerable Hogarth memorabilia, and a substantial quantity of the master's prints—including several series—"The Harlot's Progress," "Marriage à la Mode," and "The Election." Among the others is one of local amusement, a satirical portrait of the Earl of Burlington and William Kent, in connection with the earl's nearby Chiswick House.

Dr. Samuel Johnson's House (17 Gough—pronounced *Goff*—Square) is a four-story Queen Anne house on a square tucked behind Fleet Street in the City, and reached by the very same alley on which the venerable Cheshire Cheese pub has its entrance. Johnson chose it in order to be near the printer of his monumental dictionary. He lived in the house between 1748 and 1759, during which time the dictionary was a major project, with half a dozen copyists working on it exclusively, in the attic. There is a photograph of that same attic in the felicitously written guidebook to the house (the author is Cecil, Lord Harmsworth). The snap was taken in 1940, just after a ferocious World War II bombing, and one realizes what a wonder the building restoration has been. There is not as much furniture, to be sure, as there must have been during Johnson's tenure, but there is a wealth of memorabilia to compensate, and a staff that takes the house and its contents very seriously.

John Keats' House (Keats Grove, Hampstead) is the most eye-filling of this group of houses. It is early nineteenth century, handsome, and full of mementoes of the gifted young artist who was only twenty-five when he died in Rome. Next door is a library full of editions of Keats' works, as well as books about the man, and portraits of him.

VERDANT LONDON: SOME HANDSOME SQUARES, PARKS AND SUBURBS

Trafalgar Square is big and bustling and beautiful: The most impressive of London's non-residential squares. And it has all the ingredients of the urban square: A landmark (the 170-foot-high Nelson pillar), playing water (the fountains are among the loveliest in London), structures of note (the National Gallery, the National Portrait Gallery and St. Martin's-in-the-Field Church with Charing Cross Railway Station a hop and a skip away). And handsome vistas: The view along Whitehall to Big Ben and Parliament is pure picture post card. A number of important, worth-remembering thoroughfares lead into and out of the square: The Strand, for entrée into the City; Northumberland Avenue, to gain the Victoria Embankment of the Thames; Pall Mall, leading into Haymarket and Piccadilly and leading toward St. James's, Green Park and Buckingham Palace; and Charing Cross Road, which passes through theaterland.

Piccadilly Circus, its central statue of Eros notwithstanding, has all of the charm of New York's Times Square. Which is to say, not much. It is London's Tourist Headquarters. The whole world passes through the circus, both British and non-British. Heaven knows how many passengers throng through its excellently run underground station per day. There are tacky quick-service restaurants all about, some legitimate theaters, the worth-knowing-about Swan & Edgar department store. Tawdry or no, Piccadilly Circus is a focal point of consequence. Walk east on Shaftesbury Avenue, from it, and you're in the theater district. Walk north on Regent Street and you're in a major shopping area. Walk south on Regent for Pall Mall and Whitehall. Walk west on Piccadilly and you're Mayfair-bound.

Soho Square is the delightful, still mostly eighteenth-century square that gave its name to the multiculture foreign quarter so conveniently adjacent to the theater district. It contains two churches, one French Protestant, the other (St. Patrick's) Catholic, dating to 1792. Several of Soho's principal streets—including Greek and Frith—lead into it from the south. All about are mostly good, albeit not necessarily cheap, restaurants serving the cuisines of Italy, France, Greece, Hungary and China.

Berkeley (pronounced *Barkley*) **Square** is mid-eighteenth century in origin, still handsomely green in its center, but now mostly mid-twentieth century, structurally. Still, some old houses remain, mostly on the west side of the square, including No. 44, designed by William Kent.

Grosvenor Square is originally eighteenth century although much of it is now neo-Georgian twentieth century. Among the neo-Georgian buildings is the former American Embassy, now an annex of the Canadian High Commission. The Americans are now housed in a decidedly contemporary Eero Saarinen building—powerfully good-looking and appropriate for the site—whose oversized eagle was the subject of controversy when the building opened in 1960. To be noted, too, is Sir William Reid Dick's statue of Franklin D. Roosevelt, who was President during World War II when the United States and Britain collaborated closely.

Belgrave Square and its neighbors are among London's prime beauty spots. Belgrave Square itself is what elegance in architecture is all about. It is a Regency gem—surrounded by fine houses on all four sides, which today house embassies (Austrian, German, Japanese and Spanish) and scholarly societies. *Eaton Square,* nearby, is a great oblong with fine terraced houses. *Cadogan* and *Chester squares* (this last heavily populated by affluent American expatriates) are similarly posh, and the streets of this area—Wilton Crescent, Belgrave Place, Chesham Place, Pont Street, to name just a few—make for meaningful walking territory.

Sloane Square in the heart of Chelsea, is of strategic importance. The King's Road leads both east and west from it, Sloane Street leads north to Knightsbridge, and Lower Sloane Street leads south in the direction of the Chelsea Embankment and the Thames. Sloane Square's landmarks include the experimental Royal Court Theatre and the Peter Jones department store.

Portman, Manchester and Cavendish squares are near neighbors, in the Wigmore Street area, north of Oxford Street. Portman Square, with a pair of modern hotels overlooking it, has precious little to remind one of its earlier centuries, save a few exceptional houses, including one, at No. 20, which was designed by Robert Adam. The center of the square, enclosed by a wrought-iron fence, remains green, and when last I inquired, only Square residents—each with his own gate key—could make use of it; the idea is the same as that of Gramercy Park in New York. Manchester

Square is east of Portman and far better preserved. Fronting it is the Wallace Collection (see Museumgoer's London; this chapter) housed in Hertford House, the square's dominant structure. Cavendish Square remains substantially eighteenth century. A pair of houses on its north side, now a convent, are joined by an arch with a bronze Madonna by Sir Jacob Epstein—very twentieth century, of course, but a handsome complement to the neoclassic mansions. Prime Minister Anthony Asquith lived at No. 20 (now a nurses' residence) and Admiral Nelson lived at No. 5 Neighborhood streets—Vere Street (with a James Gibbs-designed church), South Melton Street, Chandos Street and Mansfield Street, to name some—are eminently explorable.

Bloomsbury Square and its neighbors are dominated by the British Museum and the University of London. This is a quarter that has retained fine squares and fine streets leading from them. When you visit the museum, assuming you've a bit of sunshine, have a look at Bloomsbury Square—farthest south: *Bedford,* adjacent to the museum and the handsomest of the lot; biggish *Russell,* still with a pleasant green interior, and the Edwardian-era Russell Hotel dominating it; and—up Woburn Place to the north —*Tavistock Square.*

London parks rarely get the attention from visitors that locals give them, which is understandable, there being so much more than green spaces to inspect in such a vast city.

St. James's Park, Green Park and Buckingham Palace Gardens are the most central of the parks, and are contiguous. St. James's is bisected by a lake that serves as a bird breeding ground. Londoners enjoy the birds and the flowers on balmy days. Green Park borders on Hyde, with the Wellington Arch and Hyde Park Corner the points of contact between the two.

Hyde Park's most noted aspect is Speakers' Corner, at Marble Arch—the long-since transplanted Buckingham Palace gateway. But there is additional activity: sailing and boating on the body of water called the Serpentine; riding on Rotten Row; band concerts at the Achilles Statue.

Kensington Gardens is adjacent to Hyde Park, to its west. Originally the private gardens of Kensington Palace—to this day the
gardens' prime attraction—they now specialize in children rather
than royalty, with mini-sailboating on the Round Pond, near the
palace, and other small-fry activity. A walk around on a balmy
day is unalloyed joy.

Holland Park is the most westerly of the major parks. Its focal
point is the venerable, now partially restored Holland House.
There are pretty gardens and concerts in summer.

Regent's Park, named for the Prince Regent (later George IV)
and designed for him by John Nash, is the northernmost of the
major London parks, and probably the most popular for recrea-
tion-bent Londoners. The chief attraction is the Zoo. An aviary
unit designed by Lord Snowdon, Princess Margaret's husband,
is a high point, but the whole complex is exceptionally well laid
out, with open-space confinement areas for the big animals
and a first-rank aquarium. The late Queen Mary's beautiful rose
gardens, in the south end of the park, rate billing, too.

Battersea Park is on the south side of the Thames, just across
from Chelsea Embankment and almost diagonally opposite handsome Cheyne Walk, and flanked by the Albert and Chelsea
bridges traversing the river. There are the usual park amenities
even including a mini-zoo. But Battersea is essentially an amusement park—a Fun Fair, with roller coaster-type rides—and is as
good a place as any to see London—rich, poor, old, young—at
play.

Kew Gardens (Kew, Surrey) is a suburban destination of the first
order. These are the Royal Botanic Gardens, and the visitor is
made to understand, from the moment he arrives at the main
gate and pays his token admission fee, that botany is king at Kew.
But what makes the gardens especially interesting to the non-
botanist is that there had been still another king at Kew—
George III, who, with his prolific wife, Queen Charlotte (who
died here in 1818), spent considerable time at the still-inspect-

able brick villa known variously as the Dutch House and Kew Palace. The house is furnished in period, and with considerable Georgian memorabilia on exhibit. But even taken on their own, forgetting the presence of a royal palace, the gardens are extraordinary. Some 25,000 botanic species grow in the 300-acre area. Walk as you like (everything is labeled clearly). There are benches for rest and rumination, and the terrain is broken up with conservatories, an Orangery and various other appropriate structures. As with the other parks, a sunny day is recommended.

Hampstead Heath, in northwest London, has two important things going for it. The first is that Kenwood House (recommended both as an art museum and a stately home, on other pages) is within its verdant bounds, and the second is that from its highest point —some 400 feet—the view of central London is smashing. There are other attractions—a celebrated pub (Spaniards' Inn), playing fields, fishing ponds, paths for peaceful walks. And engaging Hampstead proper—still remarkably Georgian and villagelike— is next door.

PERIPHERAL LONDON: FIVE SUPER-STATELY HOMES

The great country house is not necessarily *way* out in the country. What is now no more than suburbia was, several centuries back, a considerable distance from town, and building territory par excellence for the rich aristocrat. A number of these fine old houses remain. Here are five especially significant ones, representing three distinct architectural eras.

Ham House (Richmond, Surrey) went up in the early seventeenth century during the reign of James I, the son of Mary Queen of Scots, who doubled in spades as James VI of Scotland. From then, until just after World War II, it remained in the hands of the Earls of Dysart and their descendants. In 1947, it was given to the National Trust; the Victoria and Albert Museum—the national museum of decorative arts—is its actual administrator. The V and A, with its special expertise, operates it skillfully. Ham was enlarged and refurnished toward the end of the seventeenth century, and what one sees today is almost all original.

The house is one of the most luxuriously furnished in England, an absolutely prime specimen of its era. One enters a galleried Great Hall hung with paintings by Reynolds, Kneller and Van Dyck, but that is only the beginning—textiles, plasterwork, wood carving, mantels, mirrors, wall coverings, parquet floors, painted ceilings, furniture, there is not an inferior piece of work in the house. And this is not a small house with but a few rooms.

Not to be missed: the Great Staircase; the Duchess' bedroom with its immense red-canopied bed; the upstairs Long Gallery with its Sir Peter Lely paintings of voluptuous ladies; and the North Drawing Room with its English tapestries, gilded chairs and a marble fireplace flanked by twisted half-columns. Tea is served in the garden in summer, and recent years have seen seasons of concerts on summer Sunday evenings.

Chiswick House (Burlington Lane, between Great West Road and Great Chertsey Road, Chiswick) is probably the greatest pure Palladian villa outside of the prototypes in the Veneto region of northern Italy. Chiswick was built in 1725 by Lord Burlington after his return from a Grand Tour where he saw the originals.

He was fascinated with the way in which Palladio had proved that the same kind of ancient houses Horace had described could be adapted to the eighteenth century. He wanted to show that they would be as appropriate in England as in Italy. He was familiar with Inigo Jones's attempts at Palladian a century earlier (with the Queen's House at Greenwich, and the Banqueting House at Whitehall, to name a pair of still-visitable examples). But the Jones Palladian style did not catch on as it might have.

Burlington tried again, and with success. Chiswick was designed by William Kent—the multitalented landscapist-cabinet-maker-architect—in collaboration with Lord Burlington. It is smallish, and today it is largely unfurnished, more's the pity. But Kent's elaborate ceilings and wall decorations compensate for the lack of chairs, tables, sofas, rugs and paintings.

There are three exceptionally striking chambers: The Red Velvet Room, the Blue Velvet Room, and the loveliest of the lot, the central gallery, with a white-and-gold color scheme. The gardens are exceptional too. Chiswick was not intended as a residence but rather as a place to entertain. It passed from Lord Burlington to the Dukes of Devonshire, who often hosted royalty—including Czars of Russia—at Chiswick. The seventh Duke entertained Edward VII, as Prince of Wales, who spent several summers there with his family. The current landlord is the Department of the Environment, whose on-the-scene personnel are cordial and knowledgeable.

Osterley Park (near Osterley Underground station, on the Great West Road, Middlesex) is the earliest of several Robert Adam-designed country houses in the London area. A Grand Tour alumnus, Adam was an admirer of Palladio, but he considered that earlier neo-Palladian design in England, as exemplified by Inigo Jones and later William Kent, was too heavy in style, too close to the Renaissance, with elaborate coffered ceilings and other large-scale architectural details. Adam wanted lightness and more elegant proportions. His goal was "delicacy, gaiety, grace and beauty"—hardly immodest, but Adam attained it.

Osterley Park was one of his first projects. He began work on it in 1761 and didn't finish until nearly two decades later, concurrently undertaking other jobs. Like Ham, Osterley is a National Trust property—the Earl of Jersey gave it to the Trust in 1949—and also like Ham it has the good fortune to be administered by the Victoria and Albert Museum. Few houses as old as this one are as remarkably intact. Osterley's principal rooms are just as Adam created them, and that includes the furniture he had made especially for each.

The V and A people have been meticulous with details, even explaining in their excellent guidebook that "furniture was arranged in a highly formal manner with each piece standing against the wall, where it served more as a complement to the architecture than for any practical purpose." And they have left it that way: "From an inventory made in 1782, we know exactly which pieces stood in each room. . . ."

The entrance hall stuns with its magnificence—a ballroom-size, high-ceilinged chamber with the decoration consisting solely of the gray-and-white-marble floor and the plasterwork on the walls and ceiling, in Wedgwood blue and white. There is a severely beautiful, very masculine library, a dining—or "eating"—room where a series of console tables placed against the walls (with the chairs) take the place of a conventional dining table; a long, long Gallery with pale green walls to match the furniture in the same hue, and a richly embellished Tapestry Room in which tapestries cover the walls as would wallpaper.

Syon House (Brentford, Middlesex) has never, in all of its four centuries-plus, altered its stern gray Tudor facade. It is named for a convent established on the site in the early fifteenth century by King Henry V. But the house was built by the Duke of Somerset, protector of the realm during the brief reign of Edward VI, Henry VIII's son. Young Edward was the first of many celebrated visitors to enjoy Syon's hospitality through the centuries. Lady Jane Grey, who reigned as Queen of England for nine days before her beheading, was offered the crown at Syon.

In 1647, Cromwell and a host of his contemporaries met at Syon, where they made the decision that resulted in Cromwell marching his army into London and occupying the Tower and Westminster. Queen Anne, before her accession, stayed at Syon after a quarrel with her sister, Queen Mary. By the mid-eighteenth century, Syon had become the seat of the Dukes of Northumberland (which it still is). In 1762 the twelfth duke and his duchess decided it was time for a change, *within* at least.

They hired Robert Adam, who had started work at Osterley Park only a year earlier, to transform the interior of Syon while retaining the Tudor facade. Of course he succeeded. The entrance hall, obviously influenced by that at Osterley Park, is similar to it, except even larger, more impressive, and painted entirely in pale, pale gray, the only other hue being the black tiles of the checkerboard marble floor. The State Rooms are less severe and more opulent than Osterley's. The Anteroom, with its black marble pillars supporting gold neoclassic statues that in turn support a gilded ceiling, is an eye-opener. The less formal Red Drawing Room is dazzling, and so is its art: painting after painting by Lely and Van Dyck. And the Long Gallery, books lining its pale green walls, an exceptionally intricate Adam ceiling over the whole, is nothing less than sublime.

Kenwood (Hampstead Lane, Hampstead) is the latest of our trio of London-area Adam-designed houses. Lord Mansfield, its then owner, retained Adam in 1764—at the peak of his career—to transform an old house into an Adam-fashionable one. That he did, and with his usual skill and grace. Kenwood is capacious and so are its grounds. Adam transformed the house into one of symmetric elegance, with the State Room leading off an oblong entrance hall into two equally proportioned wings. The detailing is minute. The Library, with its arched ceiling supported by Corinthian columns, is the show-place room of the house.

But Kenwood is more than a house-museum. It is an art gallery of consequence. Lord Iveagh, the Guinness Brewing magnate, bought the house in 1925, installing his superlative collection of master paintings and specifying in his will that the house and its art collection (see Museumgoer's London) were to be made available to the public. Kenwood is administered by the Greater London Council.

A SELECTION OF DAY-LONG EXCURSIONS FROM LONDON

Not until you consider the possibilities of one-day excursions out of town do you realize how convenient it is to be headquartered in the capital of such a compact country. The destinations are almost limitless. One need only consult British Railways' timetable to realize how many worthwhile destinations can be comfortably visited in the span of a single day. What follows are a dozen suggestions, based on trips that I have made and enjoyed tremendously. They break down into half a dozen towns and half a dozen stately homes.

Bath: The Romans made of it a spa, naming it for its still-therapeutic waters. Medieval Britons adorned it with what is perhaps the most ingeniously proportioned mini-cathedral in Europe. The era of the first four Georges brought great architect-designers—principally the John Woods, Senior, and Junior, social dictator

Beau Nash, and VIP house renters ranging from Jane Austen to Thomas Gainsborough to George IV's Mrs. Fitzherbert.

What remains is an essentially Georgian town, which seems wisely to have allowed nearby Bristol to dominate in spheres commercial and industrial. Beau Nash would not be happy with today's masses of visitors munching Bath buns with their morning coffee or sandwiches with their afternoon tea in his beloved Pump Room. But Bath lives off the tourist trade—and treats it well.

On a day's visit out of London—good trains make this effortless —one might spend the morning visiting the Pump Room, the Roman Spa, lovely Bath Abbey, and other central destinations like Robert Adam's Pulteney Bridge spanning the Avon, broad Pulteney Street and Milsom Street with its antique and silver shops.

Lunch might well be at the Hole in the Wall, one of the best of out-of-London restaurants, with afternoon devoted to the quiet splendor of the Circus, the neighboring Royal Crescent and the more distant, more elevated Landsdown and Camden Crescents, with panoramic vistas of the town below.

The Assembly Rooms, bombed during World War II, have been skillfully restored by Oliver Messel and house the exceptionally extensive Moore Costume Collection. There are, too, the Banqueting Room of the Guildhall, the treasures of the Holbourne of Menstrie Museum, colonnaded Bath Street and Duke Street with its fine stone houses. And on structures at every turn are plaques identifying ages-past residents.

Brighton is easy to reach by train—just under an hour with departures frequent and non-stop from Victoria Station, as anyone who remembers Wilde's play, *The Importance of Being Earnest* could never forget. The south coastal resort town goes back to George IV, during the period when his father, George III, was in his declining years, mentally ill and confined to Windsor Castle, with his eldest son, the Prince Regent. "Prinny" made the town one of the most fashionable in Europe, and it remains a splendid repository of Regency architecture as well as a bathing resort.

Prinny's greatest monument is the Royal Pavilion, a glittering whimsy of a palace with an Indian Mogul facade and a quite literally dazzling interior. I should head for it post-haste upon arrival, and then be off for more of Regency Brighton—Adelaide and Lewes Crescents as a bare minimum. The great wide beaches —and the giant amusement piers which emanate from them— draw much of Britain in summer. All year round there is good shopping for antiques in the restored fishermen's houses of an engaging district called The Lanes.

There are frequent runs of pre-West End plays at the Theatre Royal. And a wide range of restaurants—Wheeler's and the Pump House among them—and many hotels of which the leaders include the Royal Crescent (Regency era) and the bigger Metropole (Victorian).

Cambridge, seat of the university that rivals Oxford for eminence, is the smaller of the two ancient university cities and without Oxford's amenities, as regards food, drink and lodging. I cannot recommend the University Arms, the major hotel, for a meal; the smaller Royal Cambridge Hotel's restaurant might be preferable. But what Cambridge lacks in that area it compensates for with the near-bucolic Cam River—the same that gave town and university their names—that runs right through it. It is easy to spend a week at Cambridge, but a good way to combine it and a nearby stately house, in a single day's excursion out of London, is to start at the university's FitzWilliam Museum—one of Britain's finest—with its exceptional Chinese pottery and jade, English glass, and paintings ranging from Rembrandt's "Man in Military Costume" to Gainsborough's "Heneage Lloyd and His Sister."

Then visit the colleges along the "Backs" of the Cam: St. John's with its Bridge of Sighs—named after the original in Venice; Magdalen, and the Restoration diaries of alumnus Samuel Pepys; ancient Peterhouse; elegant Clare; and King's, with the fan vaulting of its high, elongated Gothic chapel representing a meld of art and architecture nothing less than sublime.

Not far distant, near the little town of Bury St. Edmonds, is **Ickworth,** an early-nineteenth-century mansion that consists of a 600-foot-long rotunda whose center is punctuated by an immense 104-foot-high dome, with the curved rooms within sumptuously furnished and art-filled, and tea served on the long servants' table in the vast basement kitchen-cum-souvenir shop.

Canterbury's modern-day pilgrims outnumber those of earlier centuries, and Canterbury does not disappoint. The cathedral, seat of the Archbishop of Canterbury (resident much of the time in Lambeth Palace, his official London home), who, as primate of England is, in effect, the spiritual leader of communicants of Anglican-related churches the world over, would be eminently visit-worthy even without its spiritual or historical significance.

Still, it is worth recounting that Canterbury became a pilgrim-age town after the murder of Thomas à Becket a millennium ago. It was originally built almost a thousand years before Becket's martyrdom. The cathedral's stained glass, at least what remains of it after World War II bombing, is superlative. The Norman (Romanesque) crypt is the biggest and most impressive in the kingdom. Trinity Chapel contains the tomb of Henry IV and Edward, the Black Prince, son of Edward III. The twelfth-century choir is a treasure too. So for that matter is much of Canterbury town—bits and pieces of the ancient town walls, the Westgate, Guildhall and Royal museums; the modern University of Kent and the theater named for playwright Christopher Marlow, a son of the town. Lunch is indicated at the venerable and still good, County Hotel.

Easily visited in conjunction with Canterbury—before or on the return to London—is *Rochester,* near where Dickens died (and to which his Mr. Pickwick traveled) and in which is situated a splendid, if relatively uncelebrated, cathedral that is dominantly Norman (nave, west door, chapter house) with its newer sections early English Gothic. The evocative ruins of a Norman castle are on a hill above the town.

Oxford can comfortably be combined with what is surely the most quintessential of the English great houses, if one is selective in university sight-seeing. Concentrate, for example, on a pair of colleges—Christ Church with its awesome Gothic Dining Hall, and Trinity, with a Grinling Gibbons-carved choir in its chapel. Take in, as well, the oddly circular Sheldonian Theatre—the first if not the most beautiful of Sir Christopher Wren's works, and the site of a visitor information center for both town and university; the Bodleian Library, with its exquisite painted ceiling and illuminated manuscripts; and last, if hardly least, the treasures of the great Ashmolean Museum—Egyptian, Etruscan, Greek and later, too—with Montagna's "Virgin and Child," reason alone for an Oxford journey. There are many bigger museums in Britain; none, though, scores higher in the proportion of flawlessly beautiful objects.

One may lunch well at the in-town Randolph Hotel (there's a good grill in the basement), at the bucolic out-of-town pub known as The Trout (soup and salad lunches, Tudor breams, a trout stream) or at the ancient atmospheric—and posh—Bear Hotel in nearby Woodstock, continuing to **Blenheim.** The only non-royal house in Britain with the appellation "palace," Blenheim was given by Queen Anne, as a gift from all of her countrymen, to John Churchill, the first Duke of Marlborough, to thank him for winning the battle with the French for which the house is named. One expects Blenheim to be grand and monumental, but for architect John Vanbrugh and Capability Brown to have created a place of such style and beauty; well, these are bonuses. One look at the high-arched Long Library, the Salon's Laguerre frescoes, and the three State Rooms' tapestries, and you're willing to buck the long queues outside all over again.

Stratford-Upon-Avon is the most popular of out-of-Greater London destinations in England. There is not a visitor to the kingdom who does not know that it is Shakespeare's town—a still strongly Elizabethan place of half-timbered houses in one of which Shakespeare was born. The stellar attraction is the modern (1932) Royal Shakespeare Theatre and the first-rate production of the Bard's plays it produces. But there are other requisites, too—Ann Hathaway's house; Holy Trinity Church, where Shakespeare was baptized and buried; Hall's Croft, where his daughter lived and where contemporary exhibits are staged; Harvard House, home of the founder of Harvard University and since 1909 the university's property. Consider lunch, dinner or, indeed, an overnight stay at the strikingly handsome Stratford Hilton, or at the Welcombe or Shakespeare hotels.

Winchester is a quiet Hampshire town today, but it has known greater times. King Alfred made it England's capital a millennium ago, and its greatest monument dates from that era: an early Gothic cathedral that is the longest in all of Europe. But more important, one of the most beautiful, with its interior pillars tall, somber and in linear formation suggesting a long and elegant boulevard.

In the cathedral's library is the Winchester Bible—a medieval treasure of exceptional beauty. Winchester College, one of the kingdom's more prestigious public schools, is perhaps as celebrated as the cathedral. A good bit of it goes back to medieval times, with the Gothic chapel especially visit-worthy.

If I had but three Winchester destinations, the third would be St. Cross Hospital. It is quite as old as the cathedral and the college and was founded by a bishop to take care of a baker's dozen of indigent men. The current residents are more old than poor, but they still wear the traditional cap, gown and silver cross that their forebears wore centuries ago. And to this day, the visitor may ask for—and will indeed receive—the traditional St. Cross dole—a mug of beer and a piece of bread—that has been given to passers-by since the place was founded.

A visit to Winchester, if abbreviated, can be combined with one to Salisbury, in the same day. Or one may save Salisbury for another time and concentrate instead on the lovely Hampshire countryside, particularly the New Forest to the south. The oldest house in Winchester—Old Chesil Rectory—now sees service as a restaurant; an Italian one at that. It makes a good lunch stop. An alternative might be the venerably atmospheric White Horse Hotel in Romsey, a smallish market town not far south, with its pride a splendid nine-century-old church that had been the nucleus of an even older abbey.

Stately Homes:

Hatfield House (Hertfordshire) is as nearly requisite a stately home as the earlier-described Blenheim (see Oxford above) for reasons at once historic and esthetic. As for the former, the present house's predecessor—still standing—was the royal palace in which Henry VIII's daughter, Bloody Mary, kept her younger half-sister, the Princess Elizabeth, prisoner during part of Mary's reign. It was at Hatfield—in the old palace that now serves as a restaurant and tearoom for visitors—that Elizabeth learned of her accession to the throne.

The newer—and main—house is a perfectly beautiful early-seventeenth-century Jacobean manor built by the first Earl of Salisbury (whose descendants are still resident). Its two-story-high Great Hall—with one wall covered with a trio of Brussels tapestries and another with a carved wooden screen, is one of the superlative English rooms and is the locale of Hilliard's so-called "ermine" painting of Elizabeth I, and the Oudry portrait of her adversary, Mary Queen of Scots. Hatfield abounds in fine rooms —the King James Drawing Room with its red-and-white ceiling, and red-and-gold furniture; the 180-foot-long Long Gallery, a capacious library filled with priceless old books, and a lovely chapel with windows installed by the first earl.

Knole (Sevenoaks, Kent) could well be—indeed has been—the textbook prototype of the early English stately home: It is so very much more than simply one of the largest such structures in the country. Few houses, when all is said and done, have a pedigree so exalted, for Knole has been both the seat of an archbishop (Thomas Bourchier, mid-fifteenth-century Archbishop of Canterbury, who built it) and a royal palace (it came into Henry VIII's hands, and was inherited by his daughter, Elizabeth I). Elizabeth awarded it to one of her nobles, Thomas Sackville, the first Earl of Dorset, and the Sackvilles are still resident.

Knole, ideally, should be approached from the air so that one can appreciate, all of a piece, its vastness. It sprawls over a vast multiacre tract, a maze of vast courts, steep-chimneyed rooftops, towers, gables, turrets. The Great Staircase was the first of the expansive, showcase stairwells and set a precedent in country houses. The Great Hall, no less aptly named than the staircase, is the setting for a carved oak screen, above which bands of musicians played for Tudor balls. The Brown Gallery, with its restrained Jacobean paneling and ceiling, is at once a repository of rare paintings and equally rare furniture (Knole has one of the great furniture collections in England). And the evocatively named Venetian Ambassador's bedroom—slept in by the Doge's envoy to the Court of James I—is a chamber with tapestry-covered walls, whose canopied bed and gilded blue chairs constitute one of the kingdom's most celebrated interiors.

Luton Hoo (Luton, Bedfordshire): Any house with so memorable a name just has to be visit-worthy. Luton Hoo most certainly is. Queen Elizabeth II and Prince Philip made it a habit, at least before the 1973 death of eighty-year-old Sir Harold Wernher, to weekend at Luton Hoo, as the guests of Sir Harold and his wife, Lady Zia, at least once a year. They were most assuredly comfortable.

The house itself, begun by architect-designer Robert Adam in 1767 and set in an immense Capability Brown-conceived park, stands behind a formal turn-of-the-century rose garden. Within is an art collection worth at least $5 million. One is hard put at Luton Hoo as to whether to concentrate primarily on the house itself or its collections. The loveliest of the shown rooms are the mostly French eighteenth-century Blue Hall and a sumptuous dining room, the latter equipped with crystal and silver that had belonged to eighteenth-century English monarchs (the table is often set as for a formal dinner), with a trio of French chandeliers, and priceless Beauvais tapestries covering the walls.

The art treasures embrace furniture, porcelain, sculpture, ivories, Renaissance jewelry and Old Master paintings, including works of Italians like Lippi and Germans like Memling. A surprise —especially welcome to readers of Robert Massie's biography, *Nicholas and Alexandra,* or those who liked the book's movie version—is the basement gallery of Russian Imperial memorabilia —court dresses and family photographs, mostly—Lady Zia being a daughter of the late Grand Duke Michael of the pre-Revolution Imperial family. The restaurant is attractive.

Wilton House (Salisbury, Wiltshire), a south England treasure, is just minutes from the cathedral city of Salisbury, and is remarkable in that it embraces three disparate periods: mid-sixteenth-century Tudor, mid-seventeenth-century Inigo Jones, and early-nineteenth-century mock-Gothic. The inhabitants for some four centuries have been the Earls of Pembroke. The current Lord Pembroke, No. 17 if you want to count, is handsome, young, with a family embracing a beautiful countess and a trio of daughters—the Ladies Sophia, Emma and Flora, whom you are likely to encounter in the gardens during your inspection. The rooms to see are the half-dozen-odd designed by the school of Inigo Jones. Earlier earls entertained their sovereigns—George III and Elizabeth II to name but two—in these rooms. They are all spectacular—the little Anteroom, the Corner Room with its Rubens, Del Sarto and Lotto paintings, the Colonnade Room with works by Reynolds and Lawrence, and the chunky gilded furniture that could only be that of William Kent; and the all-round decorative inspiration of the master, Jones. Without are a spic-and-span self-service snack bar, and an interesting little shop.

One might proceed from Wilton into **Salisbury,** start here with lunch at the commendable fourteenth-century Haunch of Venison Restaurant, and then take in that town's *Cathedral,* set off on wide green lawns, and with the slim spire all the world knows through a myriad of Constable paintings. Completed in the mid-thirteenth century, Salisbury is of that Gothic that is at once somber and clean-lined, of a simplicity that surely makes it the most tranquil of England's great churches.

Within the Close—a maze of venerable streets lined with equally venerable houses surrounding the Cathedral—there are a pair of visit-worthy Queen Anne manors: one is *Malmesbury,* with an only partially exceptional interior; the other, *Montpesson,* is quite possibly the loveliest of England's smaller stately homes. Tea then—with home-baked scones, thick Devon cream and strawberry jam—at the House of Staples on the High Street, where you're positive that the lady at the next table—or perhaps the next after that—simply has to be Agatha Christie's Miss Marple.

Woburn Abbey (Bedfordshire) is one you will have heard of. Its owners and operators, the thirteenth Duke of Bedford and his French-born Duchess, run it as a high-powered, strictly commercial operation. They advertise extensively; even the grounds of the abbey contain vulgar billboards with their likenesses. The illustrated catalogue they sell to visitors contains no less than half a dozen photographs of themselves.

Besides the house itself, they run a game park—for which a separate admission is charged—filled with African animals (there are now many such in connection with stately homes, successfully designed to attract hordes of lower-class Britons who don't care a hoot about the interiors of great houses). There is, as well, a group of antique shops on the grounds, and the operators have the temerity to charge a separate admission for the privilege of looking at the wares of these commercial establishments.

Within, only a selected number of rooms are shown on the ordinary guided tours. The highly promoted dining room containing twenty-one paintings of Venice by Canaletto is generally not shown. In order to see it, the Bedfords have a scheme whereby, for a substantial sum, one can dine with them, exchanging small talk over a meal, with the Canalettos in the background. Indeed, Woburn abounds in gimmickry. The 300-year-old house is indisputably treasure filled, with such splendid interiors as the drawing, dressing and bedrooms in which Queen Victoria and Prince Albert stayed on their visits, and the Long Gallery with such priceless famous paintings as the Armada portrait of Elizabeth I, a likeness of Elizabeth's half-sister Bloody Mary, after Sir Anthony More, and a Holbein of Jane Seymour. Mind, though, the grounds, at least when last I saw them, were a mess, and I hope you will not have to make use of the facilities. The public men's room is the filthiest I have experienced in Britain, and I am advised on reliable authority that the ladies' is no less disgusting. If you go by car, Woburn may be comfortably combined in a single day with Hatfield House and Luton Hoo. A highly recommended lunch break would be at a venerable and handsomely restored inn-pub-restaurant called The Bell, that is situated in Aston Clinton, Buckinghamshire; the roast beef is superlative.

3 *London:* *To Watch*

Sitting back—more often than not, sitting forward—and watching or listening is a diversion at which London is equaled for virtuosity and variety only by New York and Paris.

Theater in this No. 1 Theater City of the World comes first with most visitors, as with so many Londoners and provincial Britons, so much so that it tends, at least with newcomers, to overshadow the musical life of the capital, which is one of the richest on the planet.

This is, as well, a major ballet center, with opera nearly as celebrated. Britain remains a major cinema-producing nation, and London offers one a chance to see films that are not exported abroad. There are variations of the French-invented *Son et Lumière* staged within the precincts of properly evocative historic settings.

Gambling is legal throughout Britain with the consequence that London is one of the very few major world capitals with smart casinos at hand. Spectator sports run an expected wide gamut—limited by no means only to traditionally British cricket and tennis.

Newcomers willing to spend the money can be surprised at the enthusiasm still shown among the locals for traditional after-dark species of urban entertainment—the night club, cabaret, dinner-dance-floor-show kind of evening. And the discothèque, its French name notwithstanding, is a British invention and still thrives.

Even a quiet evening in one's hotel room, after a strenuous day of sight-seeing, need not be a bore. In better hotels television in the rooms is as commonplace as in the United States.

THEATER AND OPERA

Theater in London goes back to the sixteenth century when the first public theater opened in Shoreditch. Its impresario was James Burbage, who came to be the employer of William Shakespeare, when the Bard left Stratford to become an actor in the capital. Shakespeare's Shoreditch experience was his first with the general kind of audience that the public theater created, and for which he became sufficiently inspired to turn from actor to playwright, with a measure of genius seldom if ever surpassed. Within a couple of decades, the same Burbage opened a new theater on the Thames' south bank—the circular Globe that achieved immortality. The London theater tradition had become entrenched.

Today, the capital has more than half a hundred theaters, one of which—the *Theatre Royal, Drury Lane*—is on the site of a predecessor that opened under Charles II's patronage more than three centuries ago. Although the rule of thumb for theatergoing in London as anywhere, is the play itself, rather than the setting, there are a handful of London theaters special enough to warrant one's at least trying to take in a production within. The Drury Lane is most certainly one such; its current home—early nineteenth century—is capacious, handsome and set behind an imposing neoclassic entrance portico. *The Theatre Royal, Haymarket,* is another similarly aged, similarly atmospheric and somewhat similarly porticoed beauty, its origins dating to the reign of George I, with its current home substantially the refurbishing of the Regent's John Nash. I think of all the London legitimate theaters it is my favorite not only because of its ambience and looks, but because I have never, as I look back, seen a bad play in it—from Wendy Hiller in *Waters of the Moon* in the early fifties, to Wendy Hiller in *Crown Matrimonial* in the early seventies. Although I cannot say that I have been as consistently lucky in offerings from its stage, I am fond, too, of the *Royal Opera House, Covent Garden.* It is a mid-nineteenth-century house, at once a place of splendor—with a red-and-gold decor, the former even including tiny, tiny crimson lampshades on panels of each of the wall sconces appended to the tiers of balconies—but still with an intimacy rarely found in the opera houses on the continent. And mind, I say this despite the decidedly regal aspects of the theater, including a royal box that has its own private supper room and a separate entrance. Not that us commoners wilt away from thirst or hunger. Covent Garden's aptly named Crush Bar provides intermission refreshment in an animated setting, and it is but one of several watering holes, all of them open a full hour before the curtain (so that you are assured of some sustenance, should you want to save dinner until afterwards), as well as during the intervals. Indeed, one may even order cold suppers—these will be served to Grand Tier Box holders and in the Crush Bar—if orders for them are placed by phone (240-1200) before 1 P.M. the day of the performance. A personal favorite, too, is the enormous, handsomely Edwardian *Coliseum,* home to the Sadler's Wells Opera (whose director in recent seasons has been musically skilled Lord Harewood—son of the late Princess Royal and a first cousin of the Queen), whose operas, it is interesting to note, are sung in English. This theater is sometimes the locale of special Royal Ballet seasons, even though the Royal Opera House is the Royal Ballet's actual home. The Coliseum is quite as adept as Covent Garden regarding the provision of nourishment. There is a wood-beamed café called the Dutch Bar in the basement and a slew of others on higher levels, with both the Dutch Bar and the Upper Circle Buffet serving cold plates; all open an hour before curtain.

Others of the more important London theaters are *Her Majesty's* and the *Palace;* they generally specialize in musicals. The *Paladium,* on the other hand, is a massive auditorium for your Judy Garland-Barbra Streisand-Liza Minelli kind of show. Of the smaller legit houses, many are attractive—the *Duke of York's,* the *New* and the *Queen's* among them. In all theaters one may have an intermission drink at the bar and, especially on matinees, have coffee and cookies served on a tray at one's seat (uncomfortable and difficult to balance, this) if the order is given in advance. Wherever he spectates in a theater, your Londoner likes his chocolates. Boxes of same are invariably on sale—the Black and White brand being the all-time favorite.

Most London theaters show productions especially produced and cast for a single run. But London has several repertory companies; indeed, it is surpassed by no city in the world in this area. The *National Theatre,* for long also called the Old Vic because its home was in the theater by that name, is the most noted (earlier members of its company included Dame Edith Evans, Sir Laurence Olivier, Vivien Leigh, Sir John Gielgud, Charles Laughton, Sir Alec Guinness—to name a few). Its home is an ultra-modern two-auditorium theater on the South Bank of the Thames, so designed to permit it to present a pair of different presentations nightly. It has a vigorous, well-thought-of junior partner, the *Young Vic.* There is, as well, the *Royal Shakespeare Company*—effectively government-subsidized as are the National Theatre and Young Vic. Its home base is the Royal Shakespeare Theatre in Stratford (see Day-long Excursions from London, Chapter 2), but it has for some time played most-of-the-year London seasons as well—at the Aldwych Theatre, until it moved to a splendidly equipped twin-auditorium home in the City's Barbican housing development. The *Royal Court Theatre,* on Sloane Square in Chelsea, is highly respected for a bold, innovative policy that has brought such playwrights as John Osborne (originally with *Look Back in Anger*) to public attention. Much earlier, a number of noted Shaw plays were first seen at the Royal Court. Its hits—including contemporary dramas by playwrights like Christopher Hampton and David Storey—often move to commercial West End theaters for extended runs.

THE ROYAL BALLET

If London holds its own with opera, it distinguishes itself with ballet. *The Royal Ballet* was born as the dance wing for the opera company originally associated with the Old Vic Theatre. When, with the advent of the thirties, the Sadler's Wells Theatre opened, the ballet took the name of the theater, and under the direction of Ninette de Valois—later awarded the title "Dame" by the Queen in recognition of her achievement—began to achieve international celebrity, to the point where it was honored by being given a permanent home just after World War II, in the Royal Opera House. Another name change—to Royal Ballet—came not long thereafter. Frederick Ashton—later knighted for his work with the company—joined Dame Ninette as the company's principal choreographer in 1935, and his successor, the current director, is Kenneth MacMillan.

All three of these balletic giants have shaped the company. The de Valois beginnings were essentially classical. Ashton carried on with that tradition (a Royal Ballet *Giselle* or *Swan Lake* is to this day a major London treat) adding his own imprint with such works as the dramatic *Daphnis and Chloe, Lady of the Camellias* —his interpretation of *Camille*—the gay and lilting *Les Patineurs* and the exuberant *Jazz Calendar*. MacMillan's major works have included a full-length *Romeo and Juliet* to music by Prokofiev, and a balletic retelling of the Anastasia story. Recent years have seen the company take the works of contemporary foreign choreographers into the repertory, including the New York City Ballet's George Balanchine (*Agon*) and Jerome Robbins (*Dances at a Gathering*). Dame Margot Fonteyn, who now dances with the company only as a guest artist upon occasion, is the best known of the company's dancers. The Soviet defector, Rudolf Nureyev —also now only an occasional guest artist—has partnered her in recent years. Male soloists of note include Antony Dowell, Desmond Kelly and David Blair, while ballerinas include Antoinette Sibley, Merle Park and Lynn Seymour. The corps de ballet is large and disciplined. The company has an auxiliary wing, The Royal Ballet New Group, and a school, whose pupils dance in public from time to time. And there is other ballet as well—the *Ballet Rambert,* for example, which performs at the Jeanette Cochrane Theatre; the *London Festival Ballet,* under the artistic direction of ex-Royal Ballet ballerina Beryl Grey; and the *London Contemporary Dance Theatre.* The Sadler's Wells Theatre is the scene of annual *International Dance Seasons* with foreign troupes performing during the spring and summer months.

CONCERTS AND RECITALS

Surely no city surpasses London within the realm of symphonic music. London has no less than five orchestras. The *Royal Philharmonic,* founded in 1813, with the Queen as its patron, has its home base in Royal Festival Hall, and never gives a concert without a bust of Beethoven on the stage. Beethoven wrote his Ninth Symphony for the orchestra and had close associations with it, as did such composers as Mendelssohn, who wrote his Fourth for the Royal Philharmonic, and Dvorak, who did likewise with his Second. The *London Symphony* is even older than the Royal Philharmonic. The *London Philharmonic,* a pipsqueak, celebrated its fortieth anniversary in 1973. Founded by the late Sir Thomas Beecham, it has in recent seasons been under the direction of the Dutchman, Bernard Haitink; its home also is Royal Festival Hall. And there are, as well, the *BBC Symphony,* and the *Philharmonia.* Not to mention the numerous chamber music groups, from the *London Mozart Players* to the *London Sinfonietta.* And symphonies from elsewhere in Britain. The *Royal Liverpool Philharmonic* and the *Bournemouth Symphony,* to name but two, make frequent London appearances, along with orchestras from abroad.

The *Royal Festival Hall* was built for the 1951 Festival of Britain on the South Bank of the Thames, near Waterloo Bridge. It is an absolutely super building, early-fifties contemporary at its very sensible, functional best, of reinforced concrete, with superb acoustics as a happy bonus. The river setting is taken advantage of with a vast terrace affording fine vistas, and above it a glass-walled restaurant—first class but reasonably priced—affording equally memorable views. There are, as well, a less expensive café, and the usual bars—these in conjunction with the vast lobby—that are a welcome fixture in British theaters. The auditorium itself is a joy. Up a level from the lobby, it seats 3,000 under a high-ceilinged roof. Adjacent, as part of the *South Bank Arts Centre,* are the smaller, also-attractive *Queen Elizabeth Hall* (with 1,100 seats) and the 370-seat *Purcell Room,* mostly for chamber music. There is, as well, the *Hayward Gallery* at which art exhibits are held regularly.

In great contrast to the Festival Hall complex is the *Royal Albert Hall,* out in Kensington, built a century ago and named for the consort of Queen Victoria, and just across the road from the al fresco memorial to him. The Royal Albert, unlike the Royal Festival, has never been loved for its acoustics. It has other things going for it, namely a capacity to seat 8,000 souls and a thousand-voice choir, all at once. Its organ is one of the biggest extant. The shape is circular—Royal Albert can be likened to a kind of fat silo. The most popular of its annual events is the series of Promenade—The Proms, to Londoners—Concerts, immodestly billed as the biggest music festival in the world, and dating back to 1895. The Proms' season is eight summer weeks, the programs star-studded, and the name appropriate, because the arena of the hall is emptied of its seats so that the audience may amble about.

Chamber music concerts and recitals are given regularly in *Wigmore Hall,* a London counterpart of New York's Town Hall and Carnegie Recital Hall. London's beautiful *churches* are frequent settings for musical events—St. Martin-in-the-Fields, on Trafalgar Square, is but one of a number. Many, particularly in the City, give lunch-time concerts, primarily for workers in the area, but with casual visitors welcome. And in summer, at least when the weather co-operates, there are *outdoor musical events* at such locales as Holland Park, the Victoria Embankment Gardens, and the Orangery of Kenwood House, Hampstead Heath.

SON ET LUMIÈRE

Son et Lumière, sound-and-light spectacles now a commonplace at historic sites the world over, have had two London locales in recent summers: the Wren-designed St. Paul's Cathedral in the City, and up the Thames in Greenwich—site of the Wren-designed Royal Naval College and the Inigo Jones-designed Queen's House, a part of the National Maritime Museum.

OUT-OF-LONDON FESTIVALS

Musical festivals are nowhere more distinguished than in Britain. Of the many, a number of the most noted, within relatively easy access from London, are the following:

Glyndbourne usually runs from late May through mid-August, and is the most fashionable and eccentric of the lot, in that the management recommends evening dress for the audience. The locale is a country house fifty-four miles from London, in the south, near Brighton, and the subject matter is opera, performed by the festival's own chorus and ballet, with music by the London Philharmonic. Dinner is served in the festival restaurants during the long intermission each evening. Glyndbourne, musically, black tie or no, is very, very high.

Cheltenham, in the Georgian spa town by that name in the Cotswolds, is under the patronage of the Duchess of Gloucester, and concerns itself heavily but by no means exclusively with British music, including newly commissioned works. It runs for a fortnight in July, with a symphony orchestra—the BBC Symphony, for example—and a variety of chamber groups and soloists.

Chichester, usually running from early May through mid-September, is a theater festival under Keith Mitchell's direction. (Previous directors had been Sir Laurence Olivier and Sir John Clements.) It usually presents four disparate dramas for the run of the season; a recent season saw works by Anouilh, Chekhov, Pinero, and Peter Ustinov, to give you an idea. The roster of resident actors is top rank, as are the directors and set designers. Chichester, easily accessible from London, is near the South Coast, between Brighton and Portsmouth. The theater's own restaurant is open before and after each performance.

Stratford-Upon-Avon's Royal Shakespeare Theatre generally operates a repertory season embracing five of the Bard's plays, from March to December. The theater is operated by a four-person team of directors—Peggy Ashcroft, Peter Brook, Peter Hall and Trevor Nunn, with Queen Elizabeth II the patron. Note that the company performs also in *London* from June to late March— most of the year in other words—at the Aldwych Theatre. During April and May, the Aldwych is the scene of an annual *World Theatre Season,* with four to six foreign companies giving performances in their own languages.

TRADITIONAL PAGEANTRY

Trooping the Colour marks the sovereign's birthday and takes place on an early June Saturday at the Horse Guards Parade. The Queen herself is the star of the show, mounted atop a royal horse. Her husband, Prince Philip, the Duke of Edinburgh, also participates, as do various units of the Royal Guard, both foot and mounted, all passing in review before Her Majesty and an audience of thousands. There is usually a dress rehearsal of the Trooping, with all present except the Queen, a day or two beforehand; the papers generally announce it.

The Royal Tournament is an annual event at Earl's Court, an immense reinforced concrete arena-exhibition hall. The tournament entrants are members of the armed forces, and the show is at once music, derring-do and pageantry, with the Queen usually present for a performance.

The State Opening of Parliament takes place early in November and embraces a glittering procession beginning at Buckingham Palace, via the Mall, Horse Guards Parade and Whitehall to the House of Lords, where the Queen reads her Speech from the Throne to both Houses, assembled in the Lords. En route, Her Majesty rides in the antique Irish State Coach.

Royal Command and Film Performances: The former is an annual charity benefit, star-studded, and with Her Majesty often in attendance, at the Palladium. The latter is another charity night, at a selected movie theater.

The Order of the Garter Ceremony is an annual June event at Windsor Castle, with the Queen leading a resplendent procession from the castle proper to St. George's Chapel.

The City of London Lord Mayor's Procession takes place the second Saturday in November; just after his election. He rides in his ancient coach from the Guildhall to the Law Courts, where the Lord Chief Justice welcomes him.

Founder's Day is an annual May event at Chelsea Royal Hospital marking the establishment of the hospital by Charles II. A parade of the red-coated pensioners precedes a special—and rather spectacular—service in the Wren-designed chapel, with traditional music by military trumpeters.

SPECTATOR SPORTS

Cricket: Lords, in St. John's Wood, usually beginning in April and running into September.

Tennis: The Wimbledon Championships are annual, early-summer events at Wimbledon's noted Lawn Tennis and Croquet Club.

Racing: To be seen at Ascot, with the dressy Royal Meetings à la *My Fair Lady* a June highlight; and Epsom, with racing in July and August.

Rowing: The Henley Royal Regatta is an annual early July event, at the Thames-side town of Henley, not far from London; the Queen is patron.

Horseback riding: The Royal International Horse Show at Wembley is an annual late-July event—show jumping is the highlight and the Queen, herself a skilled equestrienne, sometimes attends.

Croquet: The Croquet Association Open Championships, with teams from abroad competing in this very English and very ancient sport; at the Hurlingham Club.

Polo: Another popular sport in England (the Duke of Edinburgh's favorite, until fairly recently) is played at a number of clubs, including the Guards Polo Club, Windsor, and the Ham Polo Club, Surrey.

NIGHT CLUBS AND DISCOS

London persists in the *night club* tradition and makes the distinction between these establishments—which are truly membership clubs—and restaurants where there is dinner dancing and sometimes entertainment. Club memberships, usually a couple of pounds, sometimes less—are not necessary if you are taken as a guest of a member. But the tab for the evening will be high, and the course of events predictable. The *Eve Club,* 189 Regent Street, very sensibly has cheap, one-night-only memberships for foreign tourists; floor show, dancing. The *Talk of the Town* (Hippodrome Corner) is an intimate spot accommodating 700, with floor show, dancing, dinner; it's greatly popular among the locals. The big show usually goes on at 11 P.M., and the management—even more sensibly than that of the Eve—requires no membership fee at all. *Danny LaRue's,* 17 Hanover Square, is probably the best-known of the female-impersonator clubs, of which there are quite a number, for drag has always had a considerable audience in London. Danny himself is usually the star of the show.

Of the *hotels with dinner dancing,* and sometimes some entertainment, I can recommend *007* in the London Hilton (Park Lane); *Quaglino's* in the Hotel Meurice-Quaglino (Bury St.) and the *Terrace Room* of the Dorchester Hotel, (Park Lane). Worth noting, too, is *Hatchetts Piccadilly Music Hall* (67 Piccadilly)— which houses both a disco and an old-fashioned sing-along music hall, the latter cheaper and possibly more fun than the former.

The *discothèque* thrives; there are a good many, and of them the *Scotch,* in a basement off the alley called Mason's Yard, at Duke Street, *Tiffany's,* Shaftesbury Avenue, and *Knight's,* 171 Knightsbridge, are a fairly representative group.

Of the *jazz* spots, and London has quite a few, the old reliable continues to be *Ronnie Scott's,* 47 Frith Street; you listen downstairs or go upstairs, if you like, and dance in the disco; there's a membership fee.

Gambling is legal in Britain, and there are a number of London casinos. The catch is that they are operated as private clubs, and only members may play. For a foreigner to be able to gamble, he must have been a member at least 48 hours—according to British law. So if you are interested, apply at one of the clubs two days before you plan to play; take your passport with you and be prepared to pay a fairly stiff membership fee. Two clubs are

Crockfords, 16 Carlton House Terrace and *International Sporting Club,* Berkeley Square.

A NOTE ABOUT BOOKING THEATER, OPERA AND BALLET TICKETS

There are few problems here, with the exception of concerts, particularly those of symphony orchestras, in Royal Festival Hall and certain performances of the Royal Ballet and Royal Opera. The foregoing can be difficult to get seats for. Legitimate theater is usually much easier. In all cases, the most direct and cheapest way of booking is in person at the theater box-offices. If this is inconvenient, there are the booking agencies which add a not-exorbitant service charge to the cost of each ticket. The giant of the ticket-agency industry is Keith Prowse, whose head office is at 90 New Bond Street, but whose branches blanket London. Every hotel of any size has a theater-booking cubbyhole; they're usually —but not always—run by helpful ladies who frequently go out of their way to get you what you want, when you want. All of these establishments have supplies of weekly schedules of what's on in the theater, gratis. The daily press has the same information, and so do the magazines, *What's On in London, Where to Go,* and *Time Out.* Note that ticket agencies can book not only for legitimate theaters, opera, ballet and musical events, but also for seats in four or five of the major movie houses, including the Odeon Cinemas in Leicester Square, Marble Arch and St. Martin's Lane. Remember, too, that when the hotel booking offices are closed, hall porters are happy to take over and help you.

If you are *really* put together, you may want to contact the British Tourist Authority at any of its United States offices (see addresses, Chapter 7) for a current copy of their leaflet, "London Theatre: How to Get Programs and Tickets." It tells you precisely where to write for advance programs of the various opera, ballet and repertory seasons, and how to order tickets in advance from home.

4 *London: To Stay*

THE HOTEL SCENE

When a London hotel is running beautifully there is none better. Service is gracious and flawless. Everything will look well, taste good, work well. What must be borne in mind is that the better, older London hotels have had considerable experience in catering to Britain's upper classes and peerage—and there is no more knowing or demanding a clientele anywhere.

At the same time, it is well to note that one is no longer completely guaranteed an English experience in an English hotel, as used to be the case. With the exception of chefs in the better hotels' kitchens, staffs were always local, very often the sons and daughters or grandsons and granddaughters of old-timers in the same places. The ambience was English. And the language was English. Recent years have seen changes. English is not always understood, or at least well understood. The English way of doing things is sometimes more foreign to staff members with whom you come in contact than with *you*—the short-term visitors. And standards can vary. Still, managers of better hotels are doing their best to cope with vicissitudes of the employment situation. By and large, they are coping very well indeed.

The changes in staffing and services are only a part of the London hotel-scene transition. Recent seasons have seen the addition of more than three-score new hotels in London, bringing the room total to well over 17,000. But this figure bears a bit of analysis. Not a few of these hotels are designed for the group-travel business, an honorable and commendable *raison d'être*, to be sure, but with the result, frequently, the kind of ambience that is impersonal, standarized, lacking in individuality or character, and affording the kind of experience to the traveler which would not be appreciably different in similar accommodations— and mind, they do exist universally today—in Omaha or Osaka.

It is worth observing, too, that many of these new London hotels—most are in the needed middle category—are located in either fairly inaccessible and/or fairly uncharming areas, suitable perhaps for a budget traveler who has signed up for a budget tour and is willing to get about on the tour-bus which picks him up at his hotel in the morning and delivers him back there at the completion of an excursion. But not so suitable for the more curious, more sensitive traveler who enjoys being in a relatively central, more or less agreeable sector of a city so that he may walk about without difficulty, enjoying its attractions, and get to the core of town if not by foot at least by relatively uncomplicated public transport.

A word about the hall porter and other hotel staff: They have a desk of their own in virtually any hotel of size—quite separate from that of the reception clerks. Their badge is a pair of crossed keys. They are called hall porters in Britain (concierges in non-English speaking countries). They have their own professional organization, the Clefs d'Or International. And when they are good, they are wizards, and valued friends of the traveler. Of course, they keep your room key for you and take care of postage for your cards, letters and packages (which they'll have wrapped and shipped for you). But that is just routine.

You may ask the hall porter to call you a cab in hotels where they do not congregate out in front, to book you on reserved-seat trains, planes, city sight-seeing tours, or to hire guides for you; get you theater, opera, concert, ballet or sports tickets (but in hotels which have separate theater-booking offices, only at times when these offices are closed); order your favorite newspapers sent up each morning with your breakfast, even taking your order for that breakfast the night before, on your way upstairs; take care of repairs on your camera, watch, eyeglasses, shoes or business equipment; advise on restaurants, shops, barbers and hairdressers, physicians and dentists, stenographers, currently popular discos and other after-dark diversions, including those suitable (and not suitable) for women traveling alone.

Now, neither I nor the porter guarantees that you're going to approve wholeheartedly of what he recommends. But he is—or damned well should be—an experienced jack-of-all trades.

The reception clerk in the better hotels has his own desk too. He is garbed in morning dress, or a dark suit, is generally younger than the more experienced of the hall porters, is frequently Continental European (Germans appear to lead, with Swiss, Italians, Dutch and French represented too) with an amazing fluency at languages, and has—far too often—a patronizing, officious manner that is unfortunately typical of the breed, internationally.

The reception clerk, un-uniformed, considers himself a part of management, in contrast to the uniformed hall porter, down a notch on the table of organization. He is, more often than not, a recent graduate of a hotel school who has probably done considerably less traveling, and hotel checking-in than you. But he speaks four or five languages and he assumes that you don't.

He considers this a secret weapon. Moreover, he has no doubt had a good night's sleep and is fresh and rested whereas you are exhausted and disheveled after a journey that may well have included crossing an entire ocean. So, upon occasion, he may try and put one over on you—the minimum-twin you booked is unavailable, but "we have a small suite." The single you wanted was held until a few hours ago, "but you are late, we couldn't hold it any longer." Or it may be only a wait. "Have a seat in the lobby; your room will be ready in a few hours."

Chances are you will encounter none of these ploys. But be prepared; they are not uncommon, even in the very best of hotels which are otherwise excellently run, with friendly staffs. Hold your ground. Insist on what you have booked for and what has been confirmed. And if the arrogance becomes excessive, demand to speak to the general manager. You will probably be referred to a lesser official, the reception or assistant manager.

Good enough, but if satisfaction still is not obtained, ask for the Big Boss. He's back there in his office, never fear. And, after his underlings alert him to wrongdoing, he is invariably anxious to right matters, and with a smile. Or, at least, should be.

The chambermaids are the friendliest and most efficient of hotel staff, in London as all over the world. At least in the considered opinion of at least one traveler. They go about their business with no nonsense, are glad to fulfill special requests when they can (ask directly, or via a phone call to the *housekeeper*), and they are not fawning or tip-happy.

Room-service waiters run a wide gamut, particularly in London. One encounters either absolute wizards, who bring just what you ordered, in almost no time—with hot foods hot—or complete nincompoops who haven't the vaguest idea of what their jobs are all about, arrive tardily, often with something other than what has been ordered and, without the slightest subtlety, hover around waiting for a tip (even though you've been assessed a service charge for what you've ordered).

Baggage porters are generally efficient; your bags usually get to your room within a jiffy after you've checked in. They smile frequently and deserve the tips you should have ready for them.

Doormen are invariably cheerful and, if they are proficient at their jobs, they should be able to produce a taxi, even at rush hours and in the rain. Naturally, they want a tip for having done so. But a tip is hardly necessary if the cab is at the entrance and the doorman does nothing more for you than open its door.

Captains in the restaurant and lounges can be quite as patronizing as the earlier-described reception clerks. If you are going to be using the domains over which they rule with frequency, shell out early in the game.

Waiters in hotel restaurants and bars not infrequently make mistakes on the bill, rarely in your favor; check them.

Cashiers are no happier in London than in any city, to give you the small change you want when you cash a traveler's check.

They must be coaxed, and even then will attempt to give you a pile of nothing but big-denomination notes, hoping you won't know—or notice—the difference. Look them over, and if they're too big, hand them back, with a repeated request for small stuff. Chances are you won't get a smile, but you will get what you asked for. When checking out, in a big hotel, at a time that is likely to be busy, phone down half an hour or so in advance, requesting that your bill be readied; it can save time. If you will be departing at the crack of dawn, of a morning, settle your bill the night before; cashiers frequently suggest you wait until just before you leave in the morning (they would rather the cashier on duty deal with you at that time) but if you insist, they'll take your money the night before—at *your* convenience.

When all is said and done, the hotel people that are the most consistently pleasant are the *multifunction personnel*—at once receptionists, hall porters, and cashiers—who man the desks of the smaller hotels where truly personal service remains the rule.

The hotels in this book: What follows is a selection of London hotels, a personal selection, I want to emphasize, of hotels that I like, in parts of town that I consider central or agreeable or, ideally, in areas both central *and* agreeable. They run a wide gamut—luxe and grand in the great British tradition; smaller, less elaborate, more intimate, and also in the great British tradition. But there are also modern skyscrapers included in the cases of establishments where I have found service to be as kind and personal as possible, given the size and organization of the hotel. In almost every case, save one charming exception, hotels selected have a substantial number of rooms with private facilities, if not a majority, or in many cases the lot.

Still, a word about the British and the Private Bath is not out of order. Private baths in hotels until very recently—much more recently than anywhere else in Europe—were regarded as desired only by royalty and rich Martians. The realization that ordinary middle-class folk—and not only American by nationality —are accustomed to private baths with their hotel rooms, and have been for some time, is relatively recent. All of the de luxe category hotels have private baths with their rooms, even the older ones. And all the new hotels, de luxe or no, are similarly equipped. But the great group of middle-category hotels of a certain age are only just beginning to fit their bathless rooms with private facilities. So, if your goal is a hotel in this category, specify that you want a private bath. Remember, too, that the British, unlike the Scandinavians, many Continentals and the North Americans, tend to prefer tubs over showers. In many of the older hotels, a private bath still means a private b-a-t-h, not necessarily with a shower in conjunction. Once again, specify your preference.

I break down the hotels following into three broad categories: *de luxe, first class, moderate.* And I describe them on an *alphabetical* basis, within each of this trio of groupings, adding a pair of the hotels at Heathrow Airport in case overnighting there should be necessary.

SELECTED DE LUXE HOTELS

The Bristol (1 Berkeley Street) occupies the site of the old Berkeley (which made a move to Knightsbridge that, in my view, was not for the better). The Bristol's predecessor was entirely removed and an ersatz Louis XV palace substituted. The ambience is quiet. There are 200 bedrooms and seven suites. All of the accommodations are exceptionally spacious, as are the public rooms, these last including a restaurant and an adjoining lounge-bar. The location—just off Piccadilly—could not be more convenient, and if one can quarrel with the uninspired, lackluster neo-eighteenth century decor, it is at least a good deal easier to take than the contemporary plastic that might have been. A link of the Cunard chain.

Brown's (Dover Street and Albemarle Street) has been a London fixture since the year Victoria acceded to the throne. That, if you have momentarily forgotten, was 1837. It began modestly on Dover Street, soon comprising four contiguous houses. Some decades later—Victoria was in mourning at Windsor by this time—Brown's absorbed the Albemarle Hotel, on Albemarle, the street running parallel to Dover and back to back with it. By that time a foreign chap, Theodore Roosevelt by name, had checked in, object: matrimony. He was married at St. George's, Hanover Square, and a facsimile of the wedding certificate still hangs in the private-party Roosevelt Room, along with a painting of Teddy given by a daughter, and a bust of him, given by a granddaughter. Today's Brown's is remarkably like what it must have been when a Roosevelt was a resident. You enter from either Dover Street or Albemarle—both entrances are a convenient hop and a skip from Piccadilly. The old carpeted floors are evocatively creaky. There's an agreeable paneled lounge for tea or drinks, or waits for friends; an Edwardian-style cocktail lounge, traditional-decor restaurant, and 135 bedrooms and suites, almost all now with private bath (this, I sadly recall from first-hand experience, was not always the case). Many rooms have been handsomely refurbished in period style by Trust Houses-Forte, the landlords in recent years who, wisely and to their great credit, insist upon keeping Brown's quite as it has been, modern amenities the sole exception to their rule. Brown's hall porters are celebrated, and with good reason. Where does one find better, more efficient or more kind? A charmer.

The Carlton Tower (Cadogan Place-Sloane Street) once again has the name it was born with in the early sixties. (It had been, for a brief period, the Sonesta Tower but left Sonesta for Lex management, regaining its maiden name in the bargain.) Given one's preference for this part of town—smart Belgravia-Knightsbridge—the location could not be lovelier. The hotel overlooks Cadogan Place, a tree-filled square lined with handsome houses. Within pedestrian minutes are some of London's most delightful neighborhoods. But the hotel—with a nice traditional feel to its contemporary look—itself is a pleasant place to be—agreeable lobby, luxurious guest rooms (many recently refurbished), a pair of good restaurants and the relaxing Chelsea Lounge.

The Churchill (30 Portman Square) is just beyond Selfridges on Oxford Street, fronting still-green (albeit increasingly modern)

Portman Square. It was Loews Hotels' first European operation (the Hamburg Plaza in Germany—another favorite of mine—followed). Operators of de luxe New York leaders like the Regency and the Drake, they knew what they were about in the big-city hotel business. They planned carefully. The Churchill is a good-looker from the outside facade inward. Ellen Lehmann McCluskey, the New York designer who created the interiors of the Regency, crossed the Atlantic for the Churchill. Her stamp—appropriately Regency—is again evident. The rooms and suites are eye-filling, and so are the public spaces, including what has to be the most beautiful hotel coffee shop in London, not to mention the restaurant called, appropriately enough, No. 10. (There is a sculpted head of Sir Winston in the lobby.) The sunken tea lounge is a looker too. Very pleasant.

Claridge's (Brook Street) in the heart of the smartest part of Mayfair, has made a specialty of royalty over the years (since 1838, to be precise). And done very well at it. The original Claridges were a butler and his wife, a housekeeper, who had worked for the gentry. But a solitary royal signed the register in 1860, to be visited by no less grand a lady than Queen Victoria her very self. And the crowned heads have not stopped since. Commoners, though, are welcome. There is nothing distinguished about the eighteenth-century-style decor, except that it is elaborate, and that ceilings are high. Part of the staff still is liveried as in days of yore—a nice Claridge's touch this—and one drinks—tea or stronger stuff—in the lobby rather than in a detached bar on lounge, the better to watch the clientele pass in review. Accommodations are elaborate and the proportion of suites is, as one might imagine, high. There is a very big and very respectable restaurant that has never been especially noted for its cuisine, and a cheaper, informal eatery (see Chapter 5). One would not term Claridge's cozy. Comfortable, though; very comfortable.

The Connaught (Carlos Place) on still another fashionable Mayfair street, is quite as though some English friends were putting you up at their town house. Nothing French here—dark-beamed, turn-of-century, very smart English-English. Accommodations—of which there are not all that many (the total of rooms and suites is only 106)—are quietly luxe. You would not be terribly surprised to meet His Majesty, Edward VII in the paneled bar, which is in and of itself a worthy destination for the thirsty. And the restaurant warrants additional comment in Chapter 5. Very smart, albeit quiet.

The Curzon (Stanhope Row) is newish (1972), smallish (75 rooms) and modish. The style is Georgian, the bedrooms with touches of individuality in their period decor, the bathrooms marble-surfaced, and the location convenient.

The Dorchester (Park Lane) is, or at least has been for me, an extraordinary hotel experience. The luxury is the kind that English interior designers—Oliver Messel, for one—create so well, combining traditional furnishings with contemporary fabrics and colors, with the results bright and warm and welcoming. The service— reception, hall porters, waiters, barmen, chambermaids, doormen —is about as consistently good as I know of at any hotel. More on this later, but this is an exceptional place to eat, too; grill, restaurant, tea lounge, or even via room service, where a multi- course lunch or dinner is served a course at a time by the floor waiter. The ordinary bedrooms are particularly spacious. But the suites—the many regular ones and the extra-luxe Roof Garden series—are especially sumptuous. Ask for front accommodations, and your view is of Hyde Park. Quite special.

Grosvenor House (Park Lane), another Mayfair landmark, went up in the late twenties. Its architect, Sir Edward Luytens, was the very same whom the Crown had earlier commissioned to design a new capital for India when it was determined that it was time to move on from Calcutta to New Delhi, long before Indian independence was taken seriously in Whitehall. Well, if Luytens' New Delhi is now Indian, his Grosvenor House is now Trust Houses-Forte, who have put some seven million dollars into the kind of refurbishing whereby you enjoy the up-to-date quality of it all, but you still recognize the Grosvenor House you've known. The lobby is big and humming busy. The two residential wings—they are connected by the lobby and the public rooms—boast zingy accommodations. There are fine new restaurants (the late-hours Piazza is exceptional) and drinking parlors, and tea in the lounge remains a happy London pastime.

The Hyde Park (Knightsbridge) is an Edwardian dandy whose back yard is Hyde Park. (No other hotel may make that statement.) It has been masterfully refurbished to the tune of several millions over recent years—David Hicks is among the decorators—and gifted Trust Houses-Forte management has brought an ambience to the place that is one of the most winning in town—alert, animated, attractively peopled. The bedrooms and suites, many with brand-new baths, are special treats, particularly if they are at the back facing the park. There is nothing quite like being awakened each morning by the clackety-clack of Horse Guards on their way from barracks to the Admiralty, I want to tell you—and with considerable enthusiasm. Lunch in the park-view restaurant is a special treat (see Chapter 5); there are, as well, a grill and a bar-lounge, both uncommonly attractive, with clientele to match. Three Cheers.

The London Hilton (Park Lane) raised eyebrows among the locals when it opened in the early sixties—the first luxurious contemporary-design hotel of its kind in town. Muttering, muttering about those upstart colonials coming over here to run a hotel —and a skyscraper of a hotel, at that. Well, the Hilton International people pioneered in London as they have in San Juan, Addis Ababa and other parts. (There are few of their hotels anywhere in the world where I haven't stayed, and invariably with pleasure.) Their beautifully run Park Lane tower—its guest rooms are as handsome as the striking views they afford—has often been emulated, but seldom with the success of the London Hilton. And such a choice of places to eat and/or drink: To start at the top, there's a roof-top bar whose vista of London should make it a sight-seer's requisite. I am partial, also, to the eighteenth-century ambience of the lobby-floor London Tavern. And among the other eateries is one Londoners consider a favorite: the first European outpost of Trader Vic's.

The Ritz (Piccadilly) is the kind of pure, unadulterated eighteenth-century French luxury transported across *La Manche* to London, that we dream about. Exquisite is the only way to describe the look of the place. The glass-roofed pavilion called the Winter Garden—all crystal chandeliers and paneled walls and Louis XVI plasterwork—is nothing less than London's most inspired afternoon tea locale. All of the public spaces, bars, and most especially the Louis XVI Restaurant (about which more later) are quite super, and so are the bedrooms and suites.

The Savoy (Strand), in the hurly-burly, dominantly Victorian-era Strand—extending through to the Victoria Embankment on the Thames—is a good bit away from smarter Mayfair. But the location is more convenient than one might at first imagine—particularly for theater buffs and those with business in the adjacent City. And there is more than meets the eye behind the rather formidable, anything but graceful facade. Service is what has made the Savoy, although that at the Reception and Cashier's offices is no longer what it was, and can, I have learned from experience, be downright nasty. But the hall porters, on the other hand, remain kind and helpful. Room service—with waiters stationed in pantries on each floor—can be good, and accommodation varies. The bar, long a London institution, has been redone in garish contemporary style, most un-Savoy. The à-la-carte grill and the set-menu restaurant still retain their traditional decor, but at my most recent sampling, both cuisine and service in the Grill had sadly deteriorated.

The Westbury (New Bond Street) is compact, modern and operated by the New York-based Knott chain, the very same with also-good Westburys in Brussels, Toronto, Chicago, New York and San Francisco. The London variation on the Westbury theme has two major pluses: an inspired location as convenient for shops as theater, and professional service. There is a good restaurant, much frequented by Londoners, and the Polo Bar that is a trademark at each Westbury. Rooms, however, run small, although efforts have been made to redesign them so as to afford more space.

SELECTED FIRST-CLASS HOTELS

The Belgravia Royal (20 Chesham Place) is Belgravia in location, although its compact modern facade is hardly typical of
traditional Belgravia architecturally. The building occupies a
relatively small site so that public spaces are necessarily smallish,
although bedrooms—the twins if not the singles—are surprisingly
good-sized, attractive and well equipped, even extending to color
TV and phone extensions in the bathrooms. The restaurant is
a branch of Raymond Oliver's Grand Véfour, although one must
not expect anything like the atmospheric eighteenth-century original at the Palais-Royal in Paris.

The Cadogan (Sloane Street) is a handsome older house of
moderate size (there are 85 rooms, not quite all with bath) that
has recently emerged from a thorough refurbishing, Edwardian-
handsome, with super bedrooms and suites (Oscar Wilde was
arrested in one of the latter, the management advises), some of
which have extra-super new baths; a bar named for Lily Langtry,
the Edwardian actress (and Edwardian favorite) from whose
home it was taken, an elegant restaurant, and a lounge made to
order for tea or a drink. The Knightsbridge shops and Harrods
are near neighbors.

The Capital (Basil Street) has become Knightsbridge's newest
landmark, a smallish (57 rooms) hotel, with an undistinguished
modern decor, and comfortable rooms with nice extras like mini-
refrigerators to order, at no extra charge, and bathrobes for after
your shower. There is, as well, an extraordinary restaurant (see
Chapter 5), and service—reception, hall porter, restaurant, bar-
lounge—that is unsurpassed in London. But you must have the
strength to resist excessive shopping expeditions to Harrods, which
is just down the block. Exceptional.

The Cavendish (Jermyn Street), just opposite Fortnum & Mason, is a modern version of a well-known oldie that had occupied
the same space. The location is one of the most convenient in

London, with West End theaters and Mayfair equally walkable. The rooms are functional-comfortable-modern. The public areas—including a round-the-clock restaurant, of which more later, and a cozy bar—are inviting, and the service, particularly hall porter, is Trust Houses-Forte at its best.

The Charing Cross (Strand), attached to the Charing Cross Railway Station at Trafalgar Square, is a prime example of how well British Transport Hotels have spruced up their old properties. The Charing Cross is a turn-of-century souvenir of an era when things were built very grandly with high ceilings, elaborate plasterwork, palatial reception areas and huge bedrooms. British Transport has redecorated and modernized so that one enjoys all of the style of the old with contemporary facilities like private baths (most rooms now have them), inviting wine-dine facilities (see Chapter 5), and professional service.

Dukes Hotel (St. James's Place) is one you either look for or are taken to, but I'll wager it's not one you'll casually pass by; the location is just a mite out of the way for that. St. James's Place is a little cul-de-sac off central St. James's Street, closer to Pall Mall than to Piccadilly. There are less than 50 rooms (all with bath) in an Edwardian setting, with no two of them alike, a welcoming bar, a handsome and well-operated restaurant and inviting public spaces for meeting friends. Quiet, distinctive, winning.

The Europa (Grosvenor Square) is one of a number of the neo-Georgian buildings lining this handsome, originally eighteenth-century square. (A stellar exception to the rule is the decidedly contemporary American Embassy.) Still, the Europa's mock-Georgian is inoffensive. There is a capacious lobby, several inviting drinking spots and a convenient restaurant. The guest rooms are comfortable and attractive, and from Grosvenor Square one is within walking distance of the Bond and Oxford street emporia, and theaters as well.

Holiday Inn Marble Arch (George Street) is a few short blocks north of the landmark that designates it, on a quiet street running perpendicular with Edgware Road, with the department stores of

Oxford Street and the Hyde Park Speakers' Corner immediate neighbors. This is among the better-looking of the chain's ever-multiplying links, with the decor a blend of contemporary with traditional, 245 comfortable rooms, and full range of hotel amenities, including round-the-clock room service, restaurant, coffee shop and bar, as well as the every-floor ice machines that no self-respecting American motel would be without.

The Kensington Close (Wright's Lane) is a Kensington landmark —all 350 rooms of it—and, for the Kensington-bound visitor, good value. All rooms have bath and shower, and there are fine views from the upper floors, not to mention such amenities as a swimming pool, sauna, sun terrace (of *course* there is sun in Kensington), even a squash court. The Strathallan Room has a good Continental menu.

The Londonderry (Park Lane) is relatively a Johnny Come Lately among the Park Lane hostelries, which is not to say it is unwelcome. The facade is less bold than are some in the neighborhood, while the public rooms—including the restaurant-bar and coffee shop—are relaxing traditional in design, in tones of brown-beige-black, that are carried through in the guest rooms.

The Lowndes (Lowndes Street) is a newish Knightsbridge hotel with a stark, contemporary facade that does not prepare one for the interiors, which are late-twentieth-century emulations of the Georgian genius of Robert Adam. The lobby, Adam Room Restaurant and even the bedrooms are Adam style, while the bar is rather giddy Chinese Chippendale.

The Meurice-Quaglino (Bury Street) just around the corner from Jermyn Street and the rear of Fortnum & Mason (if you would like a landmark) is a winsome old-timer that has been agreeably updated. You may know the celebrated restaurant-cabaret (Quaglino's) better than the hotel. But the intimate atmosphere (there are only 41 rooms, all with bath and shower) of the hotel, along with its period-style accommodation and smiling service, are hardly to be despised, as any regular will tell you. There are a lot of same, so that booking well in advance is usually essential. Trust Houses-Forte management.

Old St. James's House (7 Park Place) is very small, very London, very atmospheric, with views from its back rooms of Green Park. There is neither restaurant nor bar, but impeccable room service —breakfast, drinks, a full meal—to compensate. This is not a hotel for anyone seeking excitement or a lobby from which to watch the world go by. There is no lobby. Only a single chair at Reception. Many of the rooms are value-packed two-room suites; they're good looking, assuming you think you will be partial to what might be described as Edwardian Art Deco. All 34 rooms and suites have bathrooms with tubs, no showers. The location— a wee dead-end street off St. James's Street—is convenient.

The Pastoria (St. Martin's Street) has the advantages of an eminently convenient Leicester Square situation, agreeable service, and an overwhelming majority of its 50-odd rooms with bath. Restaurant-bar.

The Royal Garden (Kensington High Street) is a big mid-sixties palace, with an immense high-ceilinged lobby, no less than a quartet of restaurants, an equally generous choice of bars, 500 well-planned guest rooms and suites, and most exciting, a superb situation at the edge of Kensington Gardens, with glorious views of the park below and the city beyond. There are extensive convention facilities, so plan on running into tagged delegates and spouses. Withal, given one's preference for a stay in attractive Kensington, this is among the more pleasing of the newer giants.

The Royal Horseguards (Whitehall Court) has going for it an inspired, unexpected location overlooking the Thames and near Parliament and the many lures of Whitehall. The interior is un-expected, too, for to the outer world the Royal Horseguards is a massive Victorian block, colonnaded, arched and turreted. Within, though, is a spanking new hotel: sleek-lined lobby, com-pact but good-looking red, black and white guest rooms with bath and TV; and an ice machine on every floor. Bar and coffee shop, too. One's only regret is that more of the fine original interiors were not retained when the hotel was created in the early seventies. A part of the Royal London group, whose other hotels include the Selfridge and the Royal Westminster.

The Royal Lancaster (Lancaster Terrace) is north of Hyde Park and Bayswater Road, with Marble Arch and Oxford Street some distance east. I am not especially partial to this hotel's location, but there is no denying that it is among the choicer of the new skyscrapers, with a restrained, mostly traditional decor, 467 nice-looking bedrooms and suites, a pair each of restaurants and bars, and perfectly lovely views of Hyde Park and the London beyond. A Rank hotel.

The Royal Westminster (Buckingham Palace Road) might well be called the Royal Buckingham. It is a near neighbor of the palace, to the point where the Royal Guard passes by daily en route to the Changing Ceremonies at the palace's front gate. As if that weren't saying enough for the location, it might be added that much of Central London—which is saying a lot—is within walking distance. Behind the clean-lined facade are attractive public spaces, including an inviting bar and a steak restaurant, and functional guest rooms, all with bath, shower, and television, and with ice machines on every floor. A member of the Royal London group.

The Russell (Russell Square) is the Grande Dame of Bloomsbury—a magnificent Edwardian pile, with one of the great facades of London, a marble-arched-and-pillared lobby, and a series of similarly impressive public rooms including a restaurant, a grill room, a pair of bars and a big lounge where afternoon tea—particularly welcome after a visit to the nearby British Museum——is served. The bedrooms have been modernized with uncommon style, and all now have private baths or showers, radios, and TV upon request. There is 24-hour room service, and obliging Trust Houses-Forte staff. Good value.

The Selfridge (Orchard Street) is most definitely to be confused—or at least associated—with Selfridges department store on Oxford Street. It is right next door—an inspired location for a new hotel. The Selfridge is no-nonsense modern—304 rooms with all the modern amenities—color TV, air-conditioning (not that one needs it often in London), direct-dial phones, restaurant, coffee shop, bar and—hear this, shoppers—a separate entrance of its very own to the vast, tempting department store adjoining. The flagship of the Royal London fleet.

The Sherlock Holmes (Baker Street) is included here for two reasons. The first is because it is a comfortable, medium-sized, (149 rooms) modern hotel in a reasonably convenient part of town, north of Oxford and Wigmore streets between Portman and Manchester squares. But the second is because it alone on Baker Street pays tribute to the fictional detective with whose name the street is internationally synonymous. Volumes of Holmes are on sale, there are public rooms named for the good Watson and the evil Moriarty. Note that all but a few of the bathrooms have tubs only, no showers.

The Stafford (St. James's Place, just off St. James's Street) is but a hop and a skip from Dukes (see above) and is quite as old-school and as downright charming, with a loyal army of repeat customers, again like Dukes. There are 70 rooms, all with bath (if not shower), and each with a decor quite its own. The inviting little bar has a Louis XV look. It and the adjoining restaurant (which warrants additional comment in Chapter 5) have their own (optional) entrance on Blue Ball Yard. The Stafford is a pleasure.

The Strand Palace (Strand) is value-packed. The location is the City's Strand, the exterior elderly, the interior so up to date that every one of its nearly 800 rooms has bath; there are varied eat-drink locales, including an all-you-can-eat roast beef cafeteria—see Chapter 5. And the lobby has a nice buzz to it. Part of the Strand Group.

The Tower (St. Katharine's Way) is perhaps the most imaginatively, surely the most romantically located hotel in London—on the north bank of the Thames—just across the street from Her Majesty's Tower of London, in the oldest and most historic part of town. The hotel is up-to-the-minute modern, with more than

800 futuristic rooms, and a slew of bars and restaurants, including an all-the-roast-beef-you-want Carvery. Part of the Strand Hotels chain, which includes the Strand Palace and Cumberland.

The Waldorf (Aldwych) is a landmark on the arc-shaped thoroughfare that leads off the Strand and back onto what has become Fleet Street in the City. The Waldorf is marvelously elaborate Edwardian, both without and within. Its glory is a high-ceilinged lounge (a major destination for tea or a drink), which is one of the handsomest public spaces in London. The restaurant, all crystal chandeliers and Ionic columns, is smart, and the Templars Grill is the subject of comment in Chapter 5. There are 310 bedrooms and suites which the Trust Houses-Forte management have modernized, the while happily retaining the original period style.

SELECTED MODERATE-RATE HOTELS

Moderate-category hotels in London run a wide, wide gamut, and those I have selected for this book are no exception to that rule. Indeed, a few hotels in this category could be placed in the grouping above; I list them here, though, to emphasize their good value. My standards remain high in this group, as in the previous two categories. If some of these hotels have less going for them than others, there is at least one valid reason for their inclusion —a convenient location perhaps, a goodly number of baths (still not easily come by in the cheaper London hotels), or rates that make for uncommonly solid value. As with the other categories, I have selected hotels only in neighborhoods that are pleasant.

The Basil Street (Basil Street) is so thoroughly delightful, so attractively decorated with antiques, and so agreeably located in Knightsbridge—near Harrods—that it is never wanting for clients, both domestic or imported. Indeed, you had best book way, way in advance for this one, there being no hotel in London whose regulars are more militantly enthusiastic. The Basil Street's one-flight-up lounges could be those of a great house in town or even in the country, for that matter. The restaurant is quite as good-looking, and its table-d'hôte meals are good buys. There is an even more reasonable coffee shop, very mod (see Chapter 5). Note that only about half of the 123 rooms have private baths, so be sure and specify your preference when booking.

The Bedford (Southampton Row) is a Bloomsbury favorite, particularly with visitors for whom the British Museum or the University of London are prime or frequent destination. There is a pretty garden, with the restaurant and bar overlooking it, and all of the 180-plus rooms are with bath, if not shower.

Berners Hotel (Berners Street) is an oldie, but with a fair number —nearly 90—of private baths among its nearly 240 capacious rooms. The ambience is nicely Edwardian and the location is convenient to the department stores of Oxford Street and the heart of the visitor's London just beyond.

The Bloomsbury Centre (Coram Street) is just north and east of Russell Square, in the British Museum-University of London area. It may lack atmosphere, but it is big (247 rooms and baths, all with shower) and modern, with such amenities as restaurant, coffee shop and bar-lounges.

The Clifton Ford (Welbeck Street), a functional if hardly glamorous link of the Grand Metropolitan chain, is conveniently located on Welbeck Street, a bit north of Oxford Street, near Manchester Square and the Wallace Collection. All rooms have baths, and there are a restaurant and a bar.

The Cumberland (Marble Arch) is British hotelkeeping at its moderate-level best. The idea is comfort rather than luxury, and at sensible tabs. There are more than 900 rooms, all are cheery, and all have private baths, showers and television. The lobby is big and bustling and there are several restaurants and bars, one of them exceptional, and the subject of comment in Chapter 5. The location, Oxford Street near Marble Arch, is convenient, too. Part of the Strand Group.

The DeVere (Hyde Park Gate) is a late-nineteenth-century house that has been modernized to the point where something like 80 of its 95 rooms have bath. Withal, the place remains evocatively turn of century, with views of Kensington Gardens from the better rooms—which are the ones I advise specifically requesting. There is a nice restaurant, and bar-lounge.

The Ebury Court (26 Ebury Street) is so special that even though less than half a dozen of its 35 rooms have private baths, I am including it here. It embraces a quartet of elderly joined houses. The corridors are irregular, thanks to the way the houses are joined, and the bedrooms are small but attractive, with no two alike. There is a bar open only to members who support it, but drinks are available in one of the cozy little lounges for us out-landers. The restaurant (see Chapter 5) is exceptional. Women traveling alone might bear this one in mind, at least if they don't mind stairs, for there is no elevator. The location is convenient. Victoria Station is close by and both the Piccadilly and Knights-bridge areas short bus rides away.

Flemings (Half Moon Street), just off Piccadilly, is so centrally placed that it is eternally full up, and advance booking is a req-uisite. It's elderly and attractive, but almost half of its rooms do not have private baths—worth remembering when booking.

The Green Park Hotel (Half Moon Street) is an across-the-street neighbor of Flemings, bigger, but with a smaller percentage of private baths in its smallish rooms, which are usually booked well in advance. Both are part of the Grand Metropolitan Hotels chain, with restaurants and bars in each.

The Grosvenor Court (Davies Street) is Grand Metropolitan too. I mention it because it is well situated on Davies Street, at Oxford, with Bond Street and Grosvenor Square close by. Most rooms have private bath, and there's a restaurant and bar, if not an ex-cess of charm.

The Ivanhoe (Bloomsbury Street) is a solid, no-frills, modernized hotel behind a rather forbidding facade in the British Museum area. The decor is Severe Contemporary-Functional, but the rooms—many of which have bath—are pleasant enough, the housekeeping good, and there are a moderate-priced restaurant, café and bar.

The Kenilworth (Great Russell Street) is, not unsurprisingly—given its name—an across-the-street neighbor of the above-described Ivanhoe in Bloomsbury. They are both parts of the Centre Hotels group, and they look like twins. The Kenilworth is a bit smaller than the Ivanhoe. It too has a restaurant and bar, but no coffee shop. Rates at both these Scots-plaid-decorated hostelries are identical, and so more or less are the rooms.

The Kingsley (Bloomsbury Way) is another British Museum neighbor, quiet, with a museumy-type following, and good value, with well over half of its 175 rooms equipped with private baths, if not showers. The restaurant is of the help-yourself-to-roast beef variety, and there's a bar.

The Londoner (Welbeck Street) is a same-street neighbor of the Clifton Ford; all of its 120 rooms have bath and shower, there are both a restaurant and a bar, and the location, a bit north of Oxford Street, is convenient to the big stores, Bond Street and the theaters beyond, not to mention the Wallace Collection.

The Mandeville (Mandeville Place) is still another conveniently situated moderate-category hotel. The majority of its nearly 170 rooms have bath, but not showers. There are wine-dine facilities, and Oxford and Bond streets are conveniently nearby.

The Milestone (Kensington Court) is a nice late-nineties house with vistas of Kensington Gardens, and 50 of its 80-odd rooms have private baths. Public rooms, including a restaurant and bar, remain agreeably Victorian.

The Mostyn (Portman Street) is a Portman Square-area hostelry more modest than its newer neighbors, but quite as well located, with Selfridges and the other lures of Oxford Street nearby. It's elderly, but with updated bedrooms, about half of which (out of a total of about 100) have private baths, albeit no showers.

The Mount Royal (Marble Arch) is a neighbor of the earlier-described Cumberland, and though smaller—it has but 700 rooms to the Cumberland's 900—it is competitive in that it too emphasizes no-frills comfort, at a good price, and with a convenient address. All rooms have bath, shower and TV, and there are well-priced restaurant and bar facilities.

The Normandie (163 Knightsbridge) is an oldie that has been handsomely updated, with period-decor public rooms and more contemporary bedrooms, the majority now with private baths. The bar-lounge doubles as a breakfast room, but no other meals are served, which is hardly a problem, the location being smart, restaurant-filled Knightsbridge.

The Rembrandt (Thurloe Place) is deftly tucked into the intersection of Thurloe Place and Brompton Road in Knightsbridge, as convenient to Harrods and neighboring shops as to the V and A and its neighboring museums. A unit of the Grand Metropolitan chain, it is Edwardian in origin, with the original decor happily preserved in the public rooms—these embracing a restaurant, bar and cocktail lounge. When I last saw the hotel it looked as though it could do with a bit of brightening up, but the bedrooms—especially the more than half a hundred (out of a total of about 175) with private baths—are comfortable, and there is a substantial return-clientele, much of it British.

The Rubens (Buckingham Palace Road), with its convenient opposite-the-palace location, has had a substantial refurbishing, with the result that nearly two out of three of the 150 rooms have private baths (but no showers). There is a good restaurant—popular with Londoners—and the bar, appropriately enough considering the location, is embellished with likenesses of former residents of the big house across the street.

The Rutland Court (21 Draycott Place) is just off Chelsea's Sloane Square, with Knightsbridge in one direction, and the King's Road, almost at the door. This is the small, unpretentious London hotel at its comfortable, smiling best. Only some of the 30 rooms have baths, but all are spotless and inviting, and although there is no restaurant or bar, a full English breakfast, served in one's room, is included in the room rate. And the staff could not be more obliging.

St. Ermin's (Caxton Street) provides a good example of how a late-nineteenth-century building can be converted into a serviceable late-twentieth-century hotel. All of the 252 functional rooms have their own baths and showers. The high-ceilinged, still-Victorian main lounge offers round-the-clock snack service. There's a good grill room, and a bar as well. And the location is central and convenient.

Sixteen Sumner Place (16 Sumner Place) is a small South Kensington hotel, near the Victoria and Albert Museum, with comfortable, albeit inexpensive, accommodations and attractive rates for long-term guests.

The Wilbraham (Wilbraham Place) is a perfect charmer of a Victorian hotel, all dark paneling and antique furniture, with a spic-and-span look to both public rooms (these include a good restaurant—see Chapter 5—and a bar-lounge) and guest rooms, of which there are no two alike. More than half the nearly 60 rooms have private baths (but no showers). The service is personal and pleasant; it includes breakfast served in one's room. And the location, just off Sloane Street, near Sloane Square, in Chelsea, is super.

STAYING AT HEATHROW AIRPORT

The Heathrow is clean-lined, fully equipped (color TV in the bedrooms, roast-beef restaurant, coffee shop, bar-lounge, sauna, pool) and directly on the airport grounds.

The Sheraton Heathrow is *really* up-to-date, with such gadgets as electric pants pressers and automatic drink-dispensing machines (along with color TV) in the bedrooms, and such amenities as a pool, sauna and variety of restaurants and bars, with courtesy buses (5 minutes) to the air terminal.

5   *London: To Eat (and Drink)*

THE FOOD AND DRINK SCENE

I have known English food since a few years after World War II
while I was studying in England. You still needed ration coupons
—even to eat in a university dining hall. There were precious few
eggs, the famed English beef was a sometime thing, and the Continental gastronomic influence—bless it many times over—had
not yet made inroads.

Times have changed over the years, most especially in London.
The influx of people from all over the Continent and the Commonwealth during and after World War II, for one reason or another, brought the cuisines of the Continent, and Asia, to London
in force. Coupled with that was the increase, year by year, of
Britons vacationing on the Continent—even low-income Britons
who before the war invariably stayed at home, holidaying at
Brighton, Bournemouth, Torquay or on the Cornish coast.

All of this interchange has been gastronomically beneficial. It
has created an interest in, and often a knowledge of good cooking among people of the lower classes and made it possible for
upper-class and aristocratic Britons—who, please remember, have
always eaten and drunk well—to indulge their culinary fancies
more than in the past. You have probably been told many times,
for want of too much else to say, that Britain is blessed with good
raw materials—the meat, the fruits, vegetables, the fresh fish and
shell fish. All of that is true, but no more so than in most countries
of Europe or North America.

England cooks some things very well. Roast beef, mutton and

lamb roasts and chops; roast pork, grilled bacon, mixed grill, steak and kidney pie, Dover sole, oysters, shrimps. Baked goods —cakes, pies, cookies ("biscuits" in England) and shortbreads, whole-wheat and brown breads, muffins, scones, the dessert called trifle (a kind of English *zuppa Inglese*); jams, and jellies. Cheeses, like the Cheddar and Stilton, but also lesser-known species like Wensleydale, Caerphilly, Derby, Double Gloucester and Lancashire; milk and cream, particularly the sublime clotted cream from Devon and Cornwall. Chocolates and candies. And savories: These are a category of very English dishes, traditionally (albeit rarely, nowadays) served between the dessert and cheese courses, and embracing such dishes as Welsh rarebit, mushrooms or sardines on toast, and hot buttered shrimp.

Cooked vegetables are often disastrous. Potatoes, considering how many of them are eaten, are frequently misunderstood. Gravies and sauces are best ordered on the side, except in good places. Simple things like hamburgers and hot dogs, which the British think they prepare as well as we do, can be just *terrible*. And so can attempts at Continental dishes—particularly if they are at all complex—when undertaken in the more modest places.

The best rule is to order the simplest things. Undeniably good is the traditional big breakfast: porridge, bacon—or sausage—and eggs (*always* served with a silly little grilled tomato), chilled toast (served on racks designed to expedite the chilling, better suited for letters and often used for same), and tea and coffee. Equally good—though not as easily come across these days—is afternoon tea: bread and butter, little triangles of sandwiches, perhaps hot scones and/or muffins, cake and cookies, and a pot of tea, invariably drunk with milk (not cream) and sugar.

The attractive way in which the English serve meals is never to be taken for granted. The way a table *looks* has traditionally been more important than the actual food consumed; one has only to consider the beauty of English silver, china and dining furniture over the centuries to appreciate what I mean.

As for drinks, *tea* is of course favored at teatime, and as the principal in-between pick-me-up, except at morning "elevenses," when coffee is favored, as it is also at the conclusion of dinner, and lunch as well, especially if it is a proper multicourse meal. With the middle and upper classes, by and large, coffee is generally drunk with breakfast too. The working classes and many country people still drink tea at breakfast and with their evening meal, which many still call "tea," rather than supper or dinner; such repasts are also known as "high tea," a term not to be confused with afternoon tea, no matter how elaborate it may be. When I first knew England the English swore to heaven they would *never, ever* use our insipid tea bags. Well, they have succumbed, more's the pity. If their tea—thanks to the bags—is no longer as consistently good, their *coffee* had improved, thank the good Lord, with appreciations as well to the Italians, who have taught them espresso.

The English drink quantities of room-temperature *beer*—the kind closest to ours is called lager, although hotel bars and cocktail lounges carry Danish, Dutch and German imports. But the most popular beer with the British is called "bitter"—either "ordinary" or "best." Another variety of beer is "mild"; when "mild" is combined with "bitter," the resulting concoction is called "mixed." Popular, too, is the rich brown brew called stout, made by Guinness, and not unfamiliar to Americans. Scotch *whisky* is usually just plain whisky in Britain, the nationality being implicit.

The upper classes have always been quite serious *wine* drinkers, and they are very knowledgeable about wines. Britain has for long imported more sherry than any other land. (The British very sensibly give sherry parties rather than cocktail parties, when they want to keep costs down.) It was, of course, they who gave the name sherry to the Spanish *jerez*. They drink considerably more sweet port, after dinner, than the Portuguese, who make the stuff. They are very big on table wines, mostly French. (In this connection, note that they call red Bordeaux "claret," and German white Rhine wines, "hock.") Commonwealth wines are imported too; the best by a long shot are the Australian reds, with which one does well to get acquainted.

English *gin* is as good as Scottish Scotch, and the English make their own brand of *vodka,* too. Drambuie, made with a Scotch base, is perhaps the best *liqueur* to come out of Britain. There is an enormous soft-drink industry, with Schweppes—now a familiar name in America as well—the principal make.

The *water* is everywhere drinkable, although it is a little-appreciated fact that the English appear to drink even less water than the French, or other Continental Europeans—at least in public places. English restaurants don't want to be bothered with serving a non-revenue-producing beverage like water, and water-addicted American and Canadians must often beg, and beg again, before getting their glassful.

Drinking is done in licensed restaurants, lounges, night clubs, cabarets and theaters, not to mention hotels, where guests may order in their rooms even during hours when the public bars of the hotel must be closed. Drinking is also done in the peculiar British institution known as the public house or *pub,* and sometimes—particularly in the case of those in residential neighborhoods—as the "local"; these last-mentioned serving as the adult social centers—both male and female—for their districts. (Women's lib has long been commonplace in the British pub, where the barmaid is as prevalent as the barman.) Most pubs serve the beers of but a single brewery (Ind Coope, Bass, Charrington, Courage, Watney and Worthington are among the leading makes) which double as the landlords of these retail outlets for their product. Some pubs, though, sell more than one make of brew, and are called "free houses."

Although virtually all pubs serve snacks—often a lunch-time buffet of cold, or hot and cold, snacks—some make reputations as purveyors of proper meals, served in separate, restaurant-type rooms. Both kinds of pub lunches—the buffet and the sit-down meal—are popular.

Pub hours are worth remembering. Generally, they are open from 11 A.M. to 3 P.M., and then from 6 P.M. to 11 P.M., Monday through Saturday. On Sunday, they are open only from noon to 2 P.M., and from 7:30 to 10:30 P.M. There is usually a call for the last round of drinks, and at closing, the traditional, "Time, Gentlemen, please."

About the restaurants in this book:

What follows is a *personal selection*—no more, no less—*of London restaurants, of pubs that serve good lunches, of pubs primarily for drinking, of congenial cocktail lounges, and of attractive locales for afternoon tea.* I have broken the restaurants into categories—*English-Continental, Traditional English, with a sub-category of pubs for lunch and pubs for drinks,* and *Foreign: Italian, French, Spanish, Swiss, Hungarian, Chinese, Indian, Middle Eastern* and *American.* There are, as well, sections on *Department Store* restaurants—invariably a London pleasure, and at the opposite extreme, of *Museum* cafés. In the case of each restaurant, the price range—*expensive, moderate, inexpensive*—is indicated. Telephone numbers have a way of changing, and are therefore not listed. However, bookings are recommended for all proper restaurants, including those attached to pubs. I know you realize as much as I that standards of food and service change in restaurants, in London as in any city, so that a place I have enjoyed enough to want to write about may have fallen off by the time you arrive— perhaps only temporarily—for the meal you are sampling. Conversely, restaurants about which I am not enthusiastic—and some fairly well-known ones are included here to give you an appraisal of them—may be absolutely super on those occasions when you are a customer. *Finally:* Check all bills; in no city are more mistakes made on checks of restaurants in all categories. Here we go, alphabetically within each category.

SELECTED ENGLISH-CONTINENTAL RESTAURANTS

Quibblers may quarrel with my categorization of some of the restaurants following, preferring that they be labeled as French. I consider a restaurant French only if it appears to be the genuine article (printing the menu in the French language is not quite enough). Most in London, as indeed in most non-French cities, are more French-accented than actually Gallic. Which is not necessarily to be critical, heaven knows. Indeed, the reason many of the following restaurants are included in this book is because they exemplify the culinary art of taking the best from a variety of diverse cuisines, adapting it to local tastes with the use of local ingredients, and serving it with panache and style under a single roof. Of all the major restaurant categories, this is the one that has most improved in recent years, thanks to the broader culinary horizons of the British people, their increased travels abroad, and the increased importation of foreign chefs, wine experts and, yes, waiters with a feel for and knowledge of Continental cuisines— their presentation as well as their taste.

Le Beurre Fondu (in the Wilbraham Hotel, Wilbraham Place at Sloane Street) is an absolute charmer—Continental and English dishes served in a Victorian atmosphere of white napery, polished dark-wood paneling, and fresh flowers. The service is agreeable, the roasts, grills and desserts very good indeed. Moderate.

The Brompton Grill (243 Brompton Road) is a Knightsbridge institution. Its limited seating capacity is its secret weapon. It is not too big for the service to be personal, and quite as important, the food to be fresh, hot, and delicious. Mr. Karonias, the ever-present proprietor, is a Greek, long resident in London with an extensive knowledge of the cuisines of France, the Continental countries, and England as well. His game dishes—pheasant, grouse, partridge when in season—are a specialty. But so are the traditional grills, the chicken specialties (including a Kiev that is no better at the National Hotel in Moscow), the fresh vegetables and the seafood. Waiters are mostly old-timers, proficient and, if they see that you are interested in and knowledgeable about food, congenial. Moderate to expensive.

Café Royal (68 Regent Street) is unsurpassed for the diner in search of splendor as regards both food and setting. The latter is turn-of-century Edwardian opulence. The former is a menu that blends the classic style of France—a duck *pâté,* for example, or *truite meunière aux pistaches*—with English specialties like bread pudding or roast lamb. The wine list is long and expert. There is a choice of rooms, with the Grill the smartest, and the Relais, whose specialties are French Provincial, perhaps the most interesting. A total dining experience. Expensive.

The Camellia (Syon Park, Brentford, Middlesex) is the perfect luncheon choice on that day you're devoting to stately homes on the periphery of London—Syon House, for example, and neighbors like Osterley Park and Chiswick. The Camellia, in Syon Park, is capacious, with bright, sunny decor, mostly Spanish waiters (are there any better in London?) and a delicious Continental cuisine—fresh asparagus, if it is in season, for a starter perhaps, and a grilled steak, or an Italian pasta dish, or broiled red mullet. Moderate to expensive.

Carrier's (2 Camden Passage, Islington) occupies two—or would two and a half be more correct?—floors of an aged Islington house. The look is understated, with considerable plant life, and a bit cramped for a place this expensive. The proprietor, Robert Carrier, is a youngish American long resident in Britain who has carved a culinary career as a cookbook author and the entrepreneur of this restaurant and a country outpost. Carrier's is the prototype of the high-style English-Continental restaurant. His dishes are interesting and often, but not always, delicious. Lunch and dinner are both table d'hôte (with lunch cheaper, of course) and the menus change every two months (so time your visits accordingly). You may start with truffled chicken salad, or a smoked trout mousse with heavy cream, to name two appetizers. Entrées include broiled Scotch sirloin steak—first rate—Indonesian lamb saté, turbot in champagne, or paupiettes of veal Parmesan—this last a first-rate choice. The pommes Dauphinois are a potato masterwork; indeed vegetables and green salads are a Carrier high point, while the desserts are a disappointment. The wine list is brief and well-priced. Service, mostly by young Italians, can be uneven, ranging from gracious to la-dee-da. Expensive, with the added cost—assuming you are staying in central London—of long taxi rides to and from Islington.

The Causerie (in Claridge's Hotel, Brook Street) has attained a certain celebrity as an inexpensive place to lunch in a fashionable Mayfair hotel. Taken that way, and no other, it fills the bill, but without graciousness. The fare is buffet, mostly cold, and mostly dull and predictable, with a few hot dishes. The waiters—on the scene to seat one and serve beverages and à la carte dishes—do not appear particularly happy with their lot in life, and so indicate. Moderate, at least if you watch the drinks and extras.

The Charing Cross Hotel Restaurant (Strand) has been beautifully restored to bring out the decorative details of a lovely Victorian room. And the food—hors d'oeuvres, pastries, cheeses, not to mention entrées—is tasty, too. Worth noting if you are in the Trafalgar Square area or have time to kill before catching a train in the adjacent station. Moderate.

The Connaught Hotel Restaurant (Carlos Place) has for long been considered one of London's very top-rank restaurants, and with good reason. It offers a menu mix not unlike the Café Royal, except that it is perhaps even more English, and the decor— Edwardian to be sure, but running to dark woods and white napery—is far less ebullient. Tempters include *assiette saucisses assorties*—a sampling of sausage, Dover sole, and what has to be England's premier dessert trolley. Precede your meal with drinks in the attractive hotel bar, from where you may order your lunch or dinner. Expensive.

The Dorchester Grill (Dorchester Hotel, Park Lane) is one of the handsomest of London restaurants and serves excellent food from an extensive, predominantly French-style menu. The seafoods and fish dishes are noted, but the steaks and roasts are equally exemplary, and the Dorchester's sweets are shockingly good. Note the wine list; it comprises an entire booklet and is one of the most comprehensive in the kingdom. Service is at once professional and friendly—that rarely found ideal combination. Note your fellow lunchers, or diners, too. This room—and the also engaging Terrace Room Restaurant—attracts one of London's most attractive crowds, both domestic and imported. Expensive.

The Ebury Court Restaurant (Ebury Court Hotel, 26 Ebury Street) is a London sleeper. The hotel of which it is a part— albeit charming—is small, Old School and with no more than half a dozen private baths. But the basement restaurant, traditional in its look if not always in its menu, is its ace in the hole, with dishes as diverse as *poule Basquaise*—chicken flamed in brandy with red and green peppers, onions and tomatoes; or escallope of veal Cordon Bleu, through to minute steak with mushroom and tomato, and a variety of omelettes so extensive that they occupy a menu card of their own. Home-baked bread is an Ebury Court specialty. The wine list, fairly extensive but not overly so, is one of the best-organized in town, and there are no less than a baker's dozen of after-dinner liqueurs available. Booking is essential. Moderate.

The Grange (39 King Street) occupies a formidable though nondescript building of indeterminate vintage, on a difficult-to-locate City street. But the search is worthwhile. The Grange is a looker —subtle tones of brown, black and white are used in the decor from walls and ceiling to table linens and china. This is a fairly big place with kind and attentive service and an inventive cuisine. Meals are set, and you have a choice of three or four courses, the latter, of course, more costly. In both cases—and this is a welcome novelty—house wine is included, as is coffee. Starters include massive baskets piled high with fresh raw vegetables served with dips, as well as crocks of pâtés and terrines. Entrées include *boeuf Bourguignonne* out of France, or a Middle-Eastern lamb kebab, or a more domestic poached salmon trout. The roast duckling with honey and orange is memorably delicious. Fun and festive; a good choice for an after-theater dinner. Expensive.

Lacy's (26 Whitfield Street) occupies a bit of the main floor and the big white-walled basement of a building on a little-known Soho street. The menu is part English, part French, part the inventions of the proprietors—an engaging couple, the English-born husband of which is chef, with his wife the hostess-captain-maître d'hôtel out front and a never-ending source of inspiration and ideas. Bill Lacy, with an impressive background that includes tuition under Escoffier himself, is expert at the cuisines from both sides of the Channel, and so is his wife who, as Margaret Costa, is one of England's respected food and cookbook writers. The menu is full of tempters—eggs en cocotte with smoked salmon and cream, or the house terrine, or Bill Lacy's own fish pâté with yogurt sauce, or salmon soup, to start; a gratin of crêpes with seafood for a fish course, entrées as conventional as *suprême de volaille,* or as novel as Persian roast duck with walnuts and pomegranate juice. Desserts are novel—hot fruit salad with Negrita rum is a noted specialty, but the lemon syllabub is lovely too. The service appears to depend upon the waiter; some are deft and courteous, others distinctly less so. The Lacys are both knowledgeable about wine, and their list demonstrates their expertise and interest. Everything is à la carte. Expensive.

Leith's (92 Kensington Park Road) is an elderly house that has been cleverly converted into restaurant use, with the decor no less original than the menu. This is a table d'hôte place, both at lunch and at dinner, with interesting selections to be made—game casseroles, for example, seafood bisques, a variety of made-on-the-premises pâtés, both meat and fish. There is a well-chosen wine list, and all told a Leith's lunch or dinner is a generally happy experience. Expensive.

The Park Restaurant (Hyde Park Hotel, Knightsbridge) is as pleasurable as one could ask at midday. The picture-window view is of the park, from the only hotel that has the park as a back yard. The room is handsome and high-ceilinged and the menu runs a gamut of French-style specialties—onion soup or the chef's pâté to start, trout simply grilled or a lobster thermidor; tournedos Rossini or roast duck. There are English dishes too—old-fashioned savories like Scotch woodcock and Welsh rarebit. The sweets are super, and the service is sweet. Expensive.

The Ribblesdale Restaurant (Cavendish Hotel, Jermyn Street) is more than a smart English-Continental restaurant with one of the most convenient addresses in town. It is, so far as I have been able to ascertain, the only first-class restaurant in central London that *absolutely never closes.* There may not be many occasions when you will want a good meal in pleasant surroundings at, say, three in the morning, but there are indeed times—earlier on at say 11 or midnight—when a nice place to go is worth knowing about, most restaurants shutting their kitchens soon after theater curtains lower and many being far enough away from the theater district to require a cab ride, at a time of night when cabs are hard to come by. The Ribblesdale runs a wide gamut from English dishes like chicken pie to a French-accented steak *au poivre*. Moderate to expensive.

The Ritz Hotel Restaurant (Piccadilly) is one of the most beautiful rooms in Europe, a generously proportioned Louis XVI chamber giving onto the hotel's walled garden, the severe black of the waiters' tails in pleasing contrast to the pale gray and ivory of the walls and ceiling and the plasterwork. If the food served is not as French as the ambience of the room, or indeed the nationality of the staff (most all of whom are from across the Channel), well, no matter. The à la carte menu is extensive. By no means every dish meets one's expectations, but enough are satisfactory to make a lunch or dinner an enjoyable experience. Soups throughout are good—especially the lobster bisque. So are French dishes like tournedos Périgourdine or *suprême de volaille,* and English favorites like chicken and mushroom pie, and the grilled mutton chop. Vegetables are fresh and not overcooked, and there is an extensive choice of desserts, not to mention wines. Service, in my view, is unsurpassed in London. Have a drink beforehand in the basement bar, or the Winter Garden. Expensive.

The Savoy Grill (Savoy Hotel, Strand) has been a principal London congregating spot for so long that it appears to be suffering from fatigue. The menu remains a mixed-bag, with both English and Continental dishes. But the skill of the chefs does not appear to be what it once was, and the service, in my experience, has gone down with it. Everything is à la carte; expensive.

The Stafford Hotel Restaurant (16 St. James's Place) is relatively little known, and a London surprise of consequence. It is not big, it is quiet of ambience and traditional in decor, almost completely French-staffed, and with both moderate-tabbed table d'hôte lunches and dinners, as well as an excellent à la carte menu, interesting French-accented dishes, but with English dishes, too, like potted shrimps, grilled turbot, and mixed grill, in contrast to, say, *potage bonne femme,* scampi Mornay, or *carré d'agneau* —with the lamb properly pink, *à la francais.* Soufflés are a Stafford specialty. The wines are sensibly priced, the waiters rapid and thoughtful, and the experience, all told, very pleasant indeed, conveying the feeling of one of the private clubs down St. James's Street or on nearby Pall Mall. Moderate if you order table d'hôte, expensive if you select from the à la carte.

SELECTED ENGLISH TRADITIONAL, INCLUDING PUB-RESTAURANTS

When all is said and done, no type of restaurant in London is more reliable than the traditional, home-grown English variety. And, very often, no type of restaurant is more fun or more atmospheric. Which is not to say that this group is foolproof. It is quite as possible to get a poor steak and kidney pie as a substandard *cassoulet Toulousain.* Included here are proper restaurants in the upper-price categories, middlers, a couple of good inexpensive places, but also some character-rich pubs that make a specialty of lunches, and that are easy on the pocketbook.

The Anchor (Bankside), on the Southwark side of the Thames, dates to Elizabethan times, although its current home is relatively recent seventeenth-century. There is a jumble of bars and eateries and an engaging mix of clientele—both foreign and domestic— all admiring vistas of the City—there's an observation platform— across the water. Choose a snack lunch or a sit-down one: the fare is pub-hearty, the ambience history-laden. Inexpensive.

The Antelope (22 Eaton Terrace) offers the economy of a pub in a smart Belgravia setting; Sloane Square is close by, but Eaton Terrace itself is a quiet residential street. At the Antelope you may lunch upstairs on roast beef, Dover sole or beef and kidney pie, with a slice of delicious apple pie with cheddar cheese, for dessert. Or, more informally, there is a tempting downstairs buffet with grilled sausages, cold cuts, and the like. Inexpensive.

The Audley (Mount Street) is a Mayfair pub and offers you a choice: the Gilded Cage in the cellar, the main-floor pub proper, and Annie's Attick upstairs. All three are amusing, congenial, and with good solid fare—the roast beef is justifiably celebrated—at sensible prices. Inexpensive to moderate.

The Baker and Oven (76 Brompton Road, opposite Harrods; and 10 Paddington Street) is what London could use more of. It is cheap, charming and capacious, with the bars upstairs, the eateries below. The gimmick is a big oven where customers can watch the bakers at work. But the food is not gimmicky: shepherd pie, steak and kidney pudding, bangers and mash (sausage and mashed potatoes to us), beer of course—for these are essentially pubs—but wine by the glass as well. Inexpensive.

Basil Street Hotel Restaurant (Basil Street, Knightsbridge). For the hotel's attributes, see Chapter 4. The restaurant is included here because it is one of the loveliest-to-look-at traditional-style dining rooms in London, and because it serves typical English fare—fried fillet of plaice, grilled liver and bacon, roast loin of pork with apple sauce—inexpensively and graciously, if not always deliciously. Both breakfast and lunch are three-course table d'hôte meals. Inexpensive. The same hotel's *Upstairs*—up a flight in the building next door, and connected to the main structure by an inner passage—is a mod-look short-order place, worth remembering for quick lunches and suppers, snacks, or an on-the-run afternoon tea. Inexpensive.

The Bunch of Grapes (Brompton Road) is an unabashedly Victorian pub in Knightsbridge, with an attractive clientele, and appealing if conventional pub-lunch fare. Inexpensive.

The Bunpenny (Brompton Road) is no more conventional than its oddball name. The look of the place is Exuberant Edwardian. It is a smallish restaurant, with a garrulous mod, young, albeit prosperous, clientele, enjoying their English-accented lunches and dinners. Inexpensive to moderate.

Carveries (Cumberland Hotel, Marble Arch; Strand Palace Hotel, Strand; Regent Palace Hotel, Piccadilly Circus; Tower Hotel, St. Katharine's Way). One of the most sensible developments in English eatery in recent years has been the bargain-tabbed help-yourself-to-roast-beef restaurant, at which a waiter serves you everything but the main course, which you collect, at a counter, with a chef to assist, and with the happy understanding that you may go back for more. Inexpensive.

The Chef and Brew Steak Houses are still another decidedly welcome addition to the budget-food scene. They are a chain of attractive, low-cost restaurants, usually occupying second-story rooms above pubs through which they are entered. The ambience is agreeable, the decor pleasant, the service by usually smiling waitresses, and the menu eminently sensible—platters of roast duck, mixed grill, roast chicken, fried plaice, all these served with potatoes and vegetables; as well as a variety of à la carte steaks, with traditional English desserts and cheeses to follow. And extraordinarily well-priced wines—French reds and whites, German whites ("hocks" to the British), Spanish and Portuguese types, even champagne. Irish coffee is a specialty, and needless to say, the choice of beers is extensive. There are more than a dozen London pubs with Chef and Brew Steak Houses attached to them. Of these, let me call five to your attention, all in tourist-trafficked locations: Pig and Whistle, 14 Little Chester Street in Belgravia—exceptionally pleasant, this; Shelleys, 10 Stafford Street—near Brown's Hotel and Piccadilly; The Charles Dickens, Strand—in the City; Holsten Restaurant, 34 Brook Street—in the heart of Mayfair; Snows, Piccadilly Circus. Inexpensive.

The Chelsea Potter (King's Road) lives up to its location—smart, very King's Road-Chelsea, with an appropriate clientele of modish neighborhood regulars, an engaging ambience and the usual pub-lunch comestibles. Inexpensive.

The Cheshire Cheese (145 Fleet Street at Wine Office Court) is one you have, of course, heard of. Every visitor has. But the glory of the Cheshire Cheese is that it is tourist-proof. There is not a locale in all of London that is more evocatively, albeit more genuinely, Olde English. The Cheshire Cheese is not modest about its credentials, as why should it be? It has operated, as it puts it, "under 15 sovereigns," beginning with Charles II, during whose reign it was *re*built. It occupies a building of its own at the corner of the narrow street that leads down to Gough Square and Dr. Johnson's house. Johnson was a Cheshire Cheese habitué. His portrait hangs in a place of honor in the Coffee Room, where one finds the Golden Book with the signatures of thousands of customers over the years. There are wine cellars in the basement, and the house embraces a jumble of engaging dining rooms. So that you don't get the idea that the only customers are foreign, note the City men who are regulars at the convivial bar, through every lunch hour until closing. To eat? The roast beef, served by the ambulatory carver from his trolley, is the star of a traditional menu, with all of the old favorites—from the steaks to the puddings—recommendable, most definitely including the mutton chops. Inexpensive.

Fiddlers Three (15 Beauchamp Place) is a simple, pleasantly got-up little Chelsea restaurant, with an abbreviated menu of English stand-bys, some much better than others. Service is cheerful, location convenient, and the price is right. Inexpensive.

Garners Steak House (Brompton Road) is among the more exemplary of countless London steak houses. This one, convenient to Harrods and other Knightsbridge lures, is good-looking and nicely staffed. It serves satisfying roast beef, tender steaks and meat pies, with French-fries that are hot, fresh, greaseless and unsoggy—too rare an occurrence in a city that is French-fry-happy. Inexpensive.

The George Inn (77 Borough High Street, Southwark) is sufficiently venerable to be a property of the National Trust. In its present form it dates to the late seventeenth century. It is the only galleried inn left in London. There are venerable rooms, still used for private parties, upstairs (you may have a look), and a beamed tavern below, where a good cold buffet is served at lunchtime. The adjoining dining room offers a set meal—that invariably includes roast beef, as well as grilled fish and such traditional dishes as roast chicken with bread sauce and beef-steak, kidney and mushroom pudding. There is always apple pie with fresh cream for dessert, or the old favorite known as treacle, if you prefer. The service is uncharming and the food more filling than delicious, but the price is unbeatable in London, which makes this a worthy lunch stopover if you are in the neighbor-hood, at Southwark Cathedral, for example. Inexpensive.

The Grenadier (18 Wilton Row) is a pub that goes back at least to the early nineteenth century, when it was called The Guards-man, and George IV was a customer. The clientele today is fashionable Belgravia, the lunches (and dinners, for that matter) are excellent, the service smiling, with the decor on military lines —old uniforms, swords and the like. Note, please, that you en-ter through Grosvenor Crescent, just off Hyde Park Corner, pass-ing by foot through Old Barrack Yard; it's easier than it sounds. Inexpensive to moderate.

The Grove (43 Beauchamp Place) is as good a place as any to pause in the midst of Beauchamp Place shopping. It's a two-story pub, with the bar downstairs—in warm weather, customers are out in front taking in the sun and the pedestrians. The engaging restaurant above specializes in straightforward meals—beef, hot pies, grilled fish, nice desserts. Inexpensive.

Lockets (Marsham Court at Marsham Street) may not look it, but its origins are seventeenth century. The menu makes the best reading of any in town (they'll let you have it if you will but ask) and points out that Vanbrugh referred to it in his play, *The Relapse,* which was the rage of the 1696 season, and in which the character of Lord Foppington announces that he will "go to din-ner at Locket's, and there you are so nicely and delicately served. . . ." You still are. The difference is that the restaurant is modern, with only a hint of the traditional, and that one is hard put to find a member of the staff who was not born on the Italian peninsula. (Indeed, the licensed owners, Gino Tecchia and Raffael Morelli,

sound more Latin than, say, Lord Foppington.) Which is not to
aver that the specialties are not still Olde English. The bill of
fare is divided into Fore-Dishes, Soups (there is included at that
point a venerable recipe for a potage known as Veal Glue),
Fishes, Removes and Made Dishes, Grills and Side Dishes, and—
on a separate card—Kickshaws (desserts, these), Savouries and
Cheeses. It is difficult to have a bad meal. One might start with
potted shrimp or smoked Scotch salmon, continue on to Cornish
crab soup with brandy, following with fried whitebait or baked
English trout with bacon, sampling kidneys with mushrooms or
jugged hare or venison, and concluding with brandy and sherry
syllabub or Cambridge burnt cream, with a savory like devils on
horseback or mushrooms on toast for the last course. More conventional steaks and grills are good too, and always available. The
clientele runs to MPs (Parliament is a neighbor) and Whitehall
types. And Lord Foppington would surely still approve of the
service. Expensive.

Maggie Jones's (6 Old Court Place at Kensington Church Street).
You are going to ask questions before you find Maggie's. But the
Kensington neighborhood is pleasant enough, and at the end of
your search is one of the most uncommonly good of the smaller
London restaurants. There are main floor and subterranean
dining rooms, both smartly simple, and the dishes are interesting
and tasty: cauliflower soup or eggs mayonnaise to start, entrées
like shepherd pie or a chicken-and-carrot pie with a topping of
mashed potatoes rather than piecrust; desserts like chocolate
mousse or apple crumble with thick cream. The house's good red
wine comes to table in big carafes; you pay only for the amount
you drink. And the bread is homemade. The service is informal
but agreeable and professional. Inexpensive to moderate.

The Rose and Crown (Old Park Lane) is a well-located pub just
off Piccadilly that has quite the atmosphere the visitor to London
wants in his public house. The decor is of past eras, bold and
without subtlety, with ample booths, for non-standees. This is a
convenient locale for a quick albeit relaxing lunch from the buffet

at the bar—cold meats, cheeses, French bread, and the like, washed down with a pint of lager. Inexpensive.

Rules (35 Maiden Lane) has been a City institution since the late eighteenth century. Its heyday, or at least one of them, was during the reign of Edward VII when His Majesty was a customer. Rules still packs them in. You may well need the services of your hotel hall porter to book you, although I like to think that during Edward VII's time it was better maintained and the food was a cut above what it is now. Still, the look of the place—old prints, carved beams, massive silver serving trolleys, overtired white-aproned waiters on the brink of retirement—could never be duplicated. It is indeed the genuine article, and if one sticks to the simpler stand-bys—roast Aylesbury duck, steak and kidney pie, mixed grill, grilled kidneys and bacon, fillet steak—one does well enough. There is always roast beef, of course, but it is not always as good as one would expect. The old-fashioned desserts are super, most especially the trifle. And the location is ideal for after-theater dinner. Moderate to expensive.

The Russell Hotel Restaurant (Russell Square) retains its turn-of-century marble columns and crystal chandeliers. The food is not superlative, but it is acceptable London restaurant fare, graciously served in a handsome and traditional setting, at excellent prices, particularly if one orders the set, four-course luncheons or dinners—entrées might be braised beef or grilled chicken—rather than from the considerably more costly à la carte menu. If one adheres to the above conditions: inexpensive.

The Samuel Pepys (Brooks Wharf, 48 Upper Thames) is another toughie to locate, but worth the effort—the City being one of the most browsable of London sectors. This is a modern pub and restaurant with more emphasis given to the restaurant than the pub. One drinks (and eats simply, if desired) in a capacious main bar on the ground floor, and the high-ceilinged dining room —Thames' view—is upstairs. Decor is neo-seventeenth century, the idea being to recreate the Restoration era which Pepys—who lived nearby—chronicled in his diary. Table d'hôte luncheons and dinners run to staples—oxtail soup, roast beef with York-shire pudding, with vegetables and potatoes, a tasty dessert mem-orably named spotted Dick, Stilton cheese, and coffee—and are as tasty as they are reasonable in price. There is an à la carte card too, with such specialties as pigeon and beefsteak pie, boiled mutton and caper sauce, and Samuel's syllabub. The service is uneven but well-intentioned, the crowd—especially at lunch—mostly people who work in the neighborhood. Inexpensive.

Templars Grill (Waldorf Hotel, Aldwych) is among the more interestingly populated—and animated—of City restaurants at lunchtime and is a distinct pleasure for after-the-theater dinner; many theaters are nearby. The location is a subterranean one in the Edwardian-era Waldorf Hotel. The walls are lined with murals telling the story of the old City. The menu is a veritable dictionary of traditional English fare—jellied eels, London particular (an old-fashioned cream-of-eel potage), peppered whitebait, shal-low fried river trout with pine kernels, turkey poult, bacon and mushroom pie, Aylesbury duckling, mixed grill, cold veal-and-ham pies, and such sweets as lemon posset and King Harry's shoestrings. In spring and early summer, when the next-door Aldwych Theatre runs its international drama festival, the Tem-plars features a dish of the country represented that night on the theater's stage. Moderate to expensive.

SELECTED SEAFOOD RESTAURANTS

M. J. Emberson (56 Shepherd Street) is a minuscule wine and oyster bar, in Mayfair near the Dorchester Hotel. Order the bivalves themselves, with a seafood bisque (these are very good indeed) and, of course, wine—sold by the glass, and with a wide and good choice. Moderate.

Manzi's (1 Leicester Street) is a no-nonsense, old-school-type seafood restaurant, with dining rooms on the main floor and in the basement, where the style is more casual, and there is counter service—worth knowing about, if you are alone. The *moules* *marinères* are very good, and so, for that matter, are the fish, Dover sole included. Moderate.

Mr. Bill Bentley's Wine and Seafood Bar (31 Beauchamp Place) is an amusingly conceived establishment, with as smart a clientele as one would imagine, given the Beauchamp Place location. The bar—featuring a great variety of wines by the glass—is on the street floor, and the dining room, serving an interesting fish/seafood menu—is one floor up. Moderate.

Overton's of St. James's (5 St. James's Street) is the kind of restaurant one sees in movies about fashionable London. The decor is traditional and very English. The size is middling; the place is not too big. The service is at once kind and professional. The clientele is substantial, with a definite U—meaning Upper Class—discernible at the tables. The traditional specialty is fish and seafood—lobster bisque, blue trout, sole Overton's, scampi en brochette, fresh Scotch salmon, dressed crab are noted Overton's dishes. Be advised that there are, these days, as many meat courses as fish—a variety of steaks and chops, mixed grill, calf's liver and bacon, to give you an idea. The desserts are English sweets at their best; I defy you to find a more delicious deep-dish apple pie with thick cream. And there are traditional savories—hot buttered shrimps, Scotch woodcock, mushrooms on toast. The cheese board is up to standard, too; so are the wines. Everything is à la carte. Moderate to expensive. (NOTE: Should you find yourself at Victoria Station, hungry and with time to kill, search out the Overton's near the entrance; same management.)

Poissonerie de l'Avenue (Sloane Avenue, behind Peter Jones department store) is a worth-remembering Chelsea eatery. The fish is fresh and prepared to order as you like it. The ambience is light and fun. And the prices are inexpensive.

Wheeler's (Duke of York Street) is one of a small group of this name. They are all excellent. Londoners who know the lot play their favorites. The Duke of York Street Wheeler's, in St. James's, occupies a building so narrow it comes close to not making sense.

There is a dining room on each of the several tiny floors and the Italian waiters negotiate the stairs and the compact areas with consummate skill. The menu is 100 per cent seafood; there are no steaks or mixed grills tucked away for nonconformists. The house specialty is oysters on the half-shell, when in season, ordered by the dozen or half-dozen, and by size, either large or medium. They are super. There are a dozen lobster dishes, scallops four ways, and no less than 25 sole dishes. One—St. Germain—is especially good; the fish is broiled with a fine covering of bread crumbs, and served with melted butter. The grilled trout—first dipped lightly in flour and then brushed in butter before going under the broiler—is superlative. So are the fried potatoes. Other Wheeler's are at 20 Dover Street, 40 Charlotte Street, and 15 Lownde Street. Moderate to expensive.

SELECTED FOREIGN RESTAURANTS

The hands-down winners in London's foreign-cuisine restaurant category are the Italians. Many have come since World War II and opened restaurants, so that the big difference between those of London and those of American cities is that London's are more authentic. (Ours in America are diluted, frequently, by a gap of several generations in the management, cooking and staffing; they are often more properly Italian-American than Italian.) There are quite a few French restaurants, but crossing the Channel appears not as easy for the French as crossing the Continent has been for the Italians. French restaurants can be good, but are rarely—even when costly—excellent. And they are almost never much fun; the French seem to try too hard in London. And I speak as a francophile who is inordinately fond of France, her people and her cuisine. The Chinese community gets bigger and bigger, and there are a number of good Chinese restaurants; wherever they go, these people are able to create their magnificent cuisine without difficulty. The Indians, Pakistanis and Bengalis are numerous, too, in London, and one finds more restaurants serving their foods here than in any country outside their subcontinent. Greek food is popular, and there are restaurants of other countries, from America to Armenia. What follows is a personal and selective sampling of foreign-cuisine restaurants.

AMERICAN

The Hard Rock Café (Piccadilly—near Hyde Park Corner) is a massive, dimly lighted, stylishly decorated room absolutely loaded with Londoners—young most of them—devouring the cuisine of their American cousins, as though there were no tomorrow. The menu is limited, to understate: Hamburgers and frankfurters pretty much describes it. But mind: They are good, which is rarely the case with our national staples in the U.K. Inexpensive.

Long Island (Escalade Building, Brompton Road at Beauchamp Place) is the home of a nice-looking restaurant occupying space in a shopping-arcade kind of building near Harrods. The menu is American-style, with hamburgers, sandwiches, pancakes predominating. Inexpensive.

ARMENIAN

The Armenian Restaurant (20 Kensington Church Street) is a big, modern-decor eatery devoted to the foods of the Middle East— *pilaus,* kebabs, a variety of lamb dishes, typical desserts and the good flat breads. The food will certainly not bowl you over, but the young staff tries hard. Moderate.

CHINESE

Dumpling Inn (15a Gerrard Street) is, to paraphrase one of Bette Davis's immortal lines, "a dump"—to look at, that is. It occupies a down-at-the-heel corner store in the Chinatown sector of Soho. If you are only two, you may have to share a cramped table, and if the place is especially jammed, you may be directed to the airless basement dining room, which I recommend against if the weather is at all warm, because there is little ventilation. Once seated, though, and once accustomed to the taciturn waiters, you place your order. Food arrives within minutes and it is some of the best Chinese food you have tasted. The regional specialty is Peking, and no matter what it is—pork or beef dumplings, grilled or steamed; scampi Peking style, grilled with garlic; shredded beef and green peppers; a dish of Chinese vegetables—it is delicious. The tea that almost automatically accompanies food in Chinese restaurants in the United States is not present; bottles of cold lager beer make a very good beverage. The bill comes itemized in Chinese, so you end trusting your hosts' abacus. And vowing to return. Moderate to expensive.

FRENCH

Capital Hotel Restaurant (Basil Street). The modest-sized restaurant of the modest-sized Capital Hotel, in Knightsbridge, is perhaps London's biggest gustatory surprise-package to the newcomer, or the visitor who has not been on the scene for the few seasons it has been open. This establishment is, in the view of at least one appraiser, the best French restaurant in town. There are far more handsome dining rooms, and far more ambitious menus in London. There are only about fifteen entrées, a trio of soups, half a dozen appetizers, a limited number of sweets. But, by and large, everything is masterfully prepared, beautifully served, delicious to taste, and—given the ambience of the restaurant—thoroughly enjoyable to eat. Crab bisque and chef's pâté are both fine starters. Among the entrées the steak *au poivre* and the roast lamb are authentically Gallic. The salads, cheese, desserts and wines are of equally high caliber. Expensive.

Chez Solange (35 Cranbourn Street) occupies parts of two floors of a mid-Soho building, and has established a niche for itself with both Londoners and visitors who flock to it after the theater. One wonders why. The management is kind, the service is friendly, to be sure. And the menu is extensive. Too extensive, in my view. Although the aim is obviously to present a bourgeois, rather than a haute cuisine—and why not?—the effort appears overambitious.

No restaurant as big as this one could possibly prepare *well* as many dishes as there are on the Solange menu. The result is food that ranges from poor to mediocre, at best. On a busy after-theater evening the crowd can be such that even with a reservation there is a compulsory table wait in the cocktail lounge; both there and in the restaurant, the decibel count is too high for relaxation. A lot of this would be more acceptable if the tabs were cheap in this exclusively à la carte restaurant; they are not. Moderate to expensive.

Le Français (269 Fulham Road) occupies stark, minimally decorated quarters, which would be of no concern if the staff made an effort to compensate for the coldness of the environment with some personal warmth and cheer. This, however, is lacking. The idea behind Le Français—and most commendable it is—is to present the foods of various regions of the mother country. Obviously, some regions work out better than others, so the visitor takes his chances on the region being presented when he makes his visit. Still, even with the most delicious of viands, the laboratory-like atmosphere of this place would seem to preclude an enjoyable meal which is, after all, what lunching or dining out in a costly place is all about. Expensive.

Le Gavroche (61 Lower Sloane Street) appears to at least one taster-and-sampler as a case of the Emperor's clothes. What, indeed, is all the fuss about in this celebrated restaurant? The setting is run-of-the-mill modern, the service is patronizing—the kind that rarely succeeds for long on home soil in France, the wines by no means flawless, and the food only fair-to-competent, albeit unexciting, and, given its high cost and the chilly ambience, hardly worth the substantial expenditure. Expensive.

La Napoule (8 North Audley Street) has a light, engaging, contemporary look, and although the food is French, the waiters are mostly Spanish—kindly and skilled, to be sure, but still not French, and therefore detracting from the Gallic atmosphere one might reasonably expect. The food is good if not extraordinary. Order the terrine du chef and the grilled red mullet. And don't pass up the pastries. Expensive.

Truffles (60 Beauchamp Place) is the genuine article, a French *charcuterie* in Chelsea. Its main thrust is the retailing of meats, sausages, salads and other tempters that *charcuteries* dispense. But it doubles as a restaurant at lunchtime only—small but choice, with a limited number of delicious specialties. Moderate.

GREEK

The Trojan Horse (3 Milner Street) is among the better of London's cheaper restaurants, nationality of cuisine notwithstanding. It is, however, nothing if not gastronomically Greek—from one's apéritif of water-clouded *ouzo* on into an hors d'oeuvre platter embracing the chunk of white goat cheese called *feta,* the stuffed vine leaves known as *dolma,* a tuna mousse, cold bean salad, and the traditional smoked fish concoction called *taramasalata.* Entrées revolve around lamb as would be expected, although the eggplant-casserole classic called *moussaka* is generally available and very tasty. No one tosses salads with more innate skill than the Italians and the Greeks; the specimens here are superlative. And the bread is good too. Wines are mostly Greek and you may, happily, select non-resinated ones; they are all moderately priced. The service is oddly unexuberant, which is to say un-Greek. But it is certainly not unkind, and it is certainly not inefficient. Inexpensive.

HUNGARIAN

The Gay Hussar (2 Greek Street) is a Soho destination of distinction: a first-rate Hungarian restaurant. The Hungarian cuisine is Eastern Europe's finest, without any doubt, and though one could never call it light and low-cal, it has other attributes. To order here are all of one's favorites—chicken paprika, *gulyás,* stuffed cabbage. The strudel is light, flaky and wickedly delicious. But this is just scratching the surface; the menu offers many dishes new to non-Hungarians. There are good Hungarian wines, reasonably priced, and thoroughly engaging Magyar service. Moderate to expensive.

INDIAN

Tandoori (153 Fulham Road) takes its name from the specially baked chicken that is perhaps the greatest culinary contribution the Moguls made to the Indian cuisine when they arrived on the subcontinent centuries ago. The restaurant features an authentic version of the chicken with jumbo shrimp similarly prepared, not to mention a wide-ranging Indian menu: a variety of curries, kebabs and other less-known dishes that are rather widely appreciated in this country, whose ties with India, the end of Empire notwithstanding, remain close. The restaurant is subterranean and more determinedly Indian in decor than many of its counterparts in the motherland. Still, the service is pleasant and a sampling of the menu can make for an offbeat gustatory experience. Moderate. (NOTE: The Tandoori of Mayfair, under the same management, is at 37a Curzon Street and, Mayfair being Mayfair, a bit more costly.)

ITALIAN

Alvaro (124 King's Road). Well, if one is going to have a meal on Chelsea's King's Road, it might as well be at Alvaro's. The look of the place, with its white stucco walls and interesting decorative accents, is agreeable enough. And the management is welcoming. The waiters, though, are not nearly as nice as the food, which can be first rate—*insalata numara* (an hors d'oeuvre embracing mozzarella cheese, tomato and anchovies sprinkled with oil and vinegar); *linguini puttanesca* (slim pasta with olives, tuna, capers and a tomato sauce); minestrone Milanese (Alvaro's variation on the great Italian soup theme); *pollo mistrale* (chicken sautéed in a white wine sauce): these are but a few examples. The desserts are more interesting than in your run-of-the-mill Italian restaurant. I recall a rich and splendid chocolate cake— the *torta del giorno*—with especial pleasure. Moderate.

Bianchi's (21a Frith Street) is perhaps a prototype of the middling Soho restaurant—neither excellent nor poor. Satisfactory, convenient if one is in the neighboroood, with cheerful service and setting and a conventional menu of antipasti, pasta in considerable variety, and a number of veal dishes, some of them good. Moderate.

La Capannina (24 Romilly Street), on a typical after-theater evening, is quite possibly the busiest, liveliest and noisiest restaurant in Soho. Which is going some. The hosts and waiters smile frequently, and the clientele, not minding the tightly packed tables a bit, have themselves a ball. The food is tasty too—*linguini al pesto,* for example, or the *saltimbocco alla Romana,* with chicken, seafood, and lamb dishes, as well. And excellent salads. Moderate.

Pulcinella (30 Old Brompton Road) occupies the site of the one-time Franco's at this South Kensington address. The welcome is warm from the moment one steps in the door, and it extends from management to waiter staff. The look is bright Italian-contemporary. Food is freshly made to order and more often than not, delicious. The antipasti are a specialty—from the traditional mixed platter through to *tonno e fagioli* and *insalata casanostra*—shrimps and raw mushrooms marinated with garlic and parsley, in oil and vinegar. The minestrone is super, and so are the pastas, especially the *fettucine all'Alfredo*—which is that rich concoction of green noodles tossed in a cream and cheese sauce. Moderate.

La Terrazza (19 Romilly Street) has an ebullient Soho buzz to it, on both of its handsome stucco-walled floors. The crowd is as intriguing here as the pasta. But one does well to order a veal dish, or one of the satisfying chicken or shrimp specialties; a meal here is the ultimate Italian experience—delicious, hearty, animated, fun. Moderate.

Tratoo (2 Abingdon Road, Kensington) is a winner, as regards setting (modish), service (attentive), and kitchen (distinguished). Antipasti, pasta, sauces, veal dishes: all are delicious. Moderate-expensive.

Verbarella (30 Beauchamp Place) is a winsome restaurant on a street of winsome restaurants—with the usual Italian specialties, most prepared well; a modish, mostly local clientele, and a reputation that insures a jam-packed scene at lunch hour. Moderate.

SPANISH

Martinez (25 Swallow Street) is, apparently, ageless. And has been since it opened in the twenties. I don't know it for anywhere near that long, but for as long as I have it has remained consistently good, occupying capacious quarters on a narrow little street just off Regent. The restaurant is what the non-Latin world envisioned as Spain four or five decades back, the same time Florida and California became inundated with Spanish-style houses. Martinez has a main-floor cocktail lounge and patio, with the big dining room above. It is a room of considerable dignity, with much tile. Oil paintings of the major Spanish cities are all about—each has a caption explaining the town's whereabouts to Twenties' diners, who were apparently ignorant of any city's existence in Spain other than Madrid. Martinez's menu is extensive, the table d'hôte lunches and dinners are actually more economical than they are Spanish. Which is not to say they are at all bad. The authentic Spanish dishes though—*paella* of course, *calamaris en su tinta, zarzuela de pescado y marisco, cazuela de merluza vasca, langosta en si aroma, arroz con pollo, pato a Sevillana*—are all on the à la carte menu, and more costly. There is an interesting cellar with good Spanish vintages dominating. The service is Old School; the waiters must surely be the same engaging, courteous Spaniards—most of them at any rate—who have been present since the opening. Viva Martinez! Inexpensive for the table d'hôte, through moderate to expensive, if you order à la carte.

SWISS

The Swiss Centre (2 New Coventry Street) is not unlike its commendable counterpart restaurants in New York, except that there are four restaurants on its premises, instead of the two in Manhattan. What is worth knowing, in this case, is that they are open until 1 A.M. (you may order as late as midnight). With their Leicester Square-Soho location, they are handy for cinema and theatergoers. There is a wide range in the quartet, from the Chesa —most costly of the group, with traditional specialties, fondue, *Berne platte, bundnerfleisch,* and the great potato dish called *rosti* —in a luxe setting, through to the popular-price, quick-service Rendezvous. The wines are Swiss and good, the decor is bright Swiss Modern, and the service is smiling Swiss-efficient. Inexpensive to moderate.

DEPARTMENT STORE EATING

Department store eating is a London treat. English department stores are far more concerned with feeding their customers than are many of their American counterparts. In most instances, the range is wide, extending from snack bars to waitress-service restaurants with adjoining cocktail lounges. Here is how I appraise the situation:

Barkers, on Kensington High Street, calls its inviting restaurant the *Penthouse,* what with its fifth-floor location. It is fully licensed and features, as well, a Cold Table Buffet at lunch, and a delicious Devon Farm Tea.

Biba (Kensington High Street) feeds its friends in the Rainbow Room—as unabashedly Art Deco-Thirties as is the rest of this outrageously amusing emporium.

Dickins & Jones, on Regent Street, has a handsome, high-ceilinged restaurant on its fourth floor; there are set and à la carte lunches, as well as relaxing afternoon teas. Very pleasant.

Fenwick (New Bond Street at Brook Street) has both a nice third-floor waitress-service restaurant, and a very good basement cafeteria, for lunch, coffee or tea on the run, with a fancy grocery adjoining.

Fortnum & Mason (both Piccadilly and Jermyn streets) has two noted restaurants. The busiest is *The Fountain* on the Jermyn Street side, eternally crowded and with good reason. Besides sandwiches and cold plates, there are the famed Fortnum ice creams. Happiness of a summer sight-seeing afternoon—I am here to tell you—is a chocolate soda with rum-raisin ice cream—and a blob of whipped cream for good measure—at Fortnum's. Alternatively, there is the *Fourth Floor Restaurant*. It is agreeable for morning coffee, light lunches, and afternoon tea and snacks. But be prepared for steep tabs.

Harrods (Knightsbridge), London's smartest department store, offers a number of eating possibilities. You begin with the *Health Juice Bar* in the food stalls on the main floor; continue up to the *Dress Circle Restaurant,* a good-looking self-service spot for coffee, afternoon tea, sandwiches and pastries, on the first floor (that's up a flight), and then move to the fourth floor where there are three restaurants ranging from the informal café in the *Way In* department to the attractive traditional-decor *Georgian Room,* with its own capacious cocktail lounge, and where one lunches very pleasantly indeed. The Carver's Cold Table—a sprawling buffet—is the specialty, but there are a variety of à la carte hot dishes and grills, delicious desserts selected from trollies, a bountiful selection of cheeses, and a well-chosen wine list, not surprising when one considers the excellent wine department in the food halls. It is advisable to book by phone—730-1234, ext. 3467.

Harvey Nichols' (Knightsbridge) basement café—its only restaurant—is easily skippable; not of the standard of the rest of the store.

John Lewis, a vast department-store neighbor of Selfridges on Oxford Street, has an attractive restaurant, reasonably priced, and fully licensed on its second floor.

Liberty, next door to Dickins & Jones on Regent Street, has a surprisingly small and modest restaurant—considering what a posh store it is—on its top floor. Still, they serve proper à la carte lunches—with several hot plates each day, as well as good sweets. And tabs are low.

Peter Jones, the massive department store on Sloane Square at King's Road, in Chelsea, has a pair of inviting restaurants on its fourth floor. The *restaurant* proper is à la carte, licensed and smart. There is, as well, the very contemporary-look *Scandinavian Buttery,* with counter service, table d'hôte lunches and afternoon teas, inexpensively priced.

Selfridges, the giant of Oxford Street, offers a wide choice of eateries. These include the self-service *Domino Room* on the ground floor, the up-a-flight waitress-service *Balcony Room* (not only for lunch but for Devon-style cream teas in the afternoon); the *Brass Rail* (for sandwiches and other hearty fare) in the main-floor food department; the fourth-floor *Top of the Shop*—a vast cafeteria— and that same floor's waitress-service, fully licensed, and most attractive *Grosvenor Room.* There are, as well, the *Orchard Restaurant,* near the food stalls on main, and in the bailiwick that is Miss Selfridge, there is the balcony coffee shop known as *The Bistro,* open lunch through tea, for inexpensive pick-me-ups. You may go broke in Selfridges, but you aren't going to go hungry.

Swan & Edgar, the London landmark at Piccadilly Circus and Regent Street, has a good-size, fully licensed *restaurant* on the fifth floor—reasonably priced for lunch and tea. There is, as well, a mod-look café in the basement called the *Buffet Car,* for quick refreshment.

SUSTENANCE IN THE MUSEUMS

By and large, restaurants and cafés in London's museums are worthy of but limited space in this book. They tend toward the grim and tacky. They include a basement joint in the *British Museum,* more of same in the *National Gallery,* a cafeteria and tearoom—both big but hardly lovely—in the *Victoria and Albert Museum,* a licensed, albeit uninviting, restaurant in the *Royal Academy,* a nondescript cafeteria-tearoom in the *National Maritime Museum,* Greenwich, and—praise be—a small but agreeable restaurant-café in the basement of the *Tate,* which should set an example for the others.

TEA AND DRINKS

Afternoon tea is no longer the occasion it used to be, not at least in busy, urban London. Country places are the best locales for the so-called cream teas—home-baked scones served with butter and jam, and pitchers of cream so rich it has to be scooped out with a spoon, and not for one's tea but as a topping on the scones. As if the butter and jam were not enough. Still, that is not to say that London is without a number of especially inviting spots for an afternoon tea break.

The *department stores'* restaurant facilities are described above. Tea is particularly pleasant—if one can get a seat—at *Harrods' Georgian Room, Selfridges' Balcony* and *Grosvenor Rooms, Peter Jones's Scandinavian Buttery, Barkers' Penthouse, Dickins & Jones's Restaurant, Swan & Edgar's* fifth-floor *Restaurant, John Lewis's* second-floor *Restaurant,* and last but hardly least, *Fortnum & Mason's* ground-floor *Fountain* and fourth-floor *Restaurant.*

The *hotels* remain the most elegant tea spots. Tea is an especial treat when taken in the Winter Garden of the *Ritz* (Piccadilly) —sandwiches and cakes, with white-glove service to match; the setting is sumptuous Louis XVI.

The *Dorchester* (Park Lane) is still another luxe locale, and you get a little more to eat.

At *Claridge's Hotel* (Brook Street), a liveried waiter will serve you in the lobby so that you can watch the passing parade.

The *Waldorf Hotel Lounge* (Aldwych)—elaborately high-ceilinged Edwardian—is an exceptionally good tea locale when you are in the City in mid-afternoon.

Grosvenor House (Park Lane) serves a tasty tea in its humming lobby; a diverting way to watch a segment of London pass in review.

Brown's Hotel (both Dover and Albemarle streets) serves afternoon tea—thin-sliced sandwiches and cakes—in its wood-paneled lounge; the atmosphere is very English and very clubby.

A classic additional tea locale is the *Ceylon Tea Centre* (22 Lower Regent Street) with the tea genuine Ceylonese (you may buy containers of it), and the place divided into an inexpensive à-la-carte cafeteria and a waitress-service restaurant with also inexpensive set teas; the latter is more relaxing.

Cocktails can be congenial in the hotel lounges. I particularly like the dark-beamed bar of the *Connaught* (Carlos Place); the *Ritz* (Piccadilly)—with drinks served both in the basement bar and the lobby-floor Winter Garden; the *Dorchester* (Park Lane); the *London Hilton* (Park Lane)—especially at the Roof Bar, with its splendid view; and the *Hyde Park* (Knightsbridge), especially in the lounge adjoining the Park Restaurant.

Pubs for drinking (as distinct from those earlier recommended for meals) are numberless. The ones I have already singled out are eminently recommendable for drinking as well as eating purposes; they constitute a select group of atmospheric spots, and it is only ambience, decor, location and atmosphere that distinguishes one pub from another. Still, there are some others that I should like to call to your attention. Here is a selection:

Dirty Dick's (202 Bishop's Gate) boasts proudly that it hasn't been cleaned up in a couple of hundred years; its spider webs are its trademarks. Wines, here, too, and an unusual upstairs bar.

The Duke of Albemarle (Dover Street) is a well-located pub for the West End visitor, on Dover at the corner of Stafford, in Piccadilly. The look is modish; the drinkers likewise.

The Grapes (Brompton Road) is a Knightsbridge watering hole, convenient to Harrods and the other attractions of this attractive section of town.

The Lamb and Flag (Rose Street) is a theater-district landmark, a happy choice for after the play. This is the West End's oldest timber-framed drinking house; dates all the way back to the Tudor era.

The Mayflower (117 Rotherhithe Street) is a timbered oldie named for the Pilgrims' ship, near the church (St. Mary's) where its captain is buried, and with a Thames view. The Pilgrims sailed from close by for England's Plymouth, thence for the Rock.

The Piccadilly Nuisance (Dover Street) is, not surprisingly, a Piccadilly pub, at the corner of that thoroughfare and Dover Street, and with a clientele of well-got-up locals melded with drop-in visitors, who know a pleasant place when they see one.

The Salisbury (St. Martin's Lane) is a between-acts drinks spot and an after-theater magnet, as well, with thespian types prevalent among the regular clientele. The look is opulent turn-of-century, with carved wood paneling and elaborate mirrors. Good eats, too.

The Sherlock Holmes (Northumberland Street) is a monument to the fictional detective, with all manner of Holmesiana, even including an imagined mock-up of his Baker Street digs. Suggested for buffs.

The Waterman's Arm (Glenaffric Avenue) is as good an example as any of the entertainment-pubs. This one—dating to Victorian times—is along the Thames docks, and comes to life in the evening with old-fashioned Variety acts, and the gang joining in. Fun.

6   *London: To Buy*

The beauty part of shopping in London is that it's all done in English. Sometimes this is not a beauty part at all; it's too easy, which can result in its becoming too costly. But shopping in the English language would not be all that worthwhile if there were not worthy wares. Believe me, there are. Not, mind you, that there are any bedrock bargains. Everything that is exported to the United States is, of course, somewhat cheaper on home ground, but not all that much.

No, it is the design and quality and variety—and the smart way in which things often are displayed and merchandised—that keep us in stores for disproportionately greater periods of our time in London than should be the case, if we want to see other aspects of the city than the insides of its emporia.

THE SHOPPING AREAS

First, though, where to shop? I would break Shopper's London down this way:

Piccadilly—between Piccadilly Circus and Green Park (moderate to expensive).

Regent Street—from Pall Mall to Oxford Street (moderately high to expensive).

Oxford Street—from Marble Arch to Charing Cross Road (moderate).

Knightsbridge—including Brompton Road, Sloane Street and Fulham Road (moderate to expensive).

King's Road, Chelsea—from Sloane Square to Beaufort Street (moderate to expensive).

Mayfair—roughly, the area bounded by Park Lane, Regent Street, Piccadilly and Oxford Street, and including Old and New Bond streets, Curzon Street and Savile Row (expensive).

Kensington—including Kensington Church and Kensington High streets (moderate to expensive).

Soho—including Shaftesbury Avenue (moderate).

Strand—from Trafalgar Square until the name changes to Fleet Street (moderate).

PROFILING THE DEPARTMENT STORES

London's deparment stores rank with those of the major North American cities and a very few other cities (Tokyo, Copenhagen, Stockholm, Paris) as among the very best on the planet. They reflect the British genius at marketing, merchandising, display and salesmanship, not to mention, more often than not, the national penchant for style and taste. For the visitor from abroad, they are an effortless lesson in the capital's—and indeed the country's—standard of living, and for that matter, life-styles. Even for the most tightfisted of travelers who have allotted nary a ten-dollar traveler's check for the shops, they are browseworthy.

Harrods, the domed brownstone palace that is Knightsbridge's chief landmark, is the undisputed top dog of the lot. Prices range from moderate to expensive. In Chapter 2 I have included Harrods' food halls as one of London's Dozen Requisites. They dominate an entire area of the main floor, and deserve your attention, although not exclusively. Elsewhere on main, consider the Men's and Boys' Shops—all-London leaders in these areas;

fabrics by the yard, silver and jewelry, the handsomest perfume-cologne department—all coral and white—in town; even a pharmacy and an interpreter's booth.

The first floor (our second) is given over to women's, girls', children's, and babies' clothing departments; there's even a youngsters' barber. And up a flight to the second, one finds many departments to interest overseas visitors, including housewares, garden equipment (the British are passionate gardeners) and books. The third floor is also of interest, with a first-rate antiques section in the furniture department, a delightful toy section, and a browseworthy and unexpected second-hand books section. Harrods' fourth floor—the top one—is the site of its major restaurants (Chapter 5), its absolutely wild Way In section—a mod department store within a department store and with its own café—a women's hairdresser, and The Trimmers—a men's barber shop. Also on four, a theater-ticket bureau and export department (worth checking with for tax concessions on large purchases), and if you please, Harrods' very own bank, which is no less surprising than the fact that Harrods has its own veterinary department for customers with sick pets, and a catering department for customers wanting help with home parties. One last tip: ladies' rooms are on the first and fourth floors; men's on the ground, second, third and fourth.

Selfridges (Oxford Street near Marble Arch) is more popular-priced than Harrods, absolutely enormous, and quite as worth knowing as the Knightsbridge store. The cavernous main floor includes a London souvenirs department—with some tasteful things among the usual junk; a well-stocked men's accessories department—sweaters, turtlenecks, shirts, ties and the like; a food department that is not as handsome to look upon as Harrods but hardly to be despised as it includes wines and a mouth-watering delicatessen; a super book department (with an especially good paperback section, for light-to-carry titles you may want to take home); a flower shop, and—especially worth noting, this—what has to be the most complete magazine-and-newspaper stand in London. A section of the main floor, with its own separate entrance, is devoted to the popular Miss Selfridge, which is almost a store by itself, specializing in young women's clothing. Then, to go down before going up, there is the vast, important-to-visitors basement, with china, glass and housewares in abundant variety. Men's clothing, as distinct from men's furnishing, is upstairs on the first floor, along with a men's barber shop. Women's and children's clothing are on two and three, and the fourth is for the major restaurants and the Export Department, for help with shipping of big purchases and possible tax rebates on same. There's a ladies' room on the second floor, with men's rooms on the first and third floors. Selfridges has more restaurants than any other London department store; consult Chapter 5.

John Lewis (Oxford Street). Of Selfridges' big neighbors on Oxford Street, John Lewis is by far the most interesting. Though less well known abroad than Selfridges, it's a favorite with Londoners, and it's a big store, extending from Oxford Street through to attractive Cavendish Square, from which it may also be entered. There is a commendable sense and style and smartness in the merchandise, beginning with the men's department in the basement (also the location of china, glass, gifts and housewares), and continuing on up to the Export Department on five. In between are young men's clothing on four, an earlier-described restaurant on two, and women's and children's clothes and accessories, staring on main and continuing a couple of floors upward.

(The other major Oxford Street department stores are *D. H. Evans,* with mostly inexpensive and not particularly interesting wares, at least for the foreign visitor; *Marshall & Snelgrove,* which is essentially a medium to inexpensive clothing store lacking éclat; and *Marks & Spencer,* of which more later, under Clothing.)

Liberty (Regent Street) is surely as requisite in the department store category as Harrods and Selfridges. It is considerably smaller than both, but quite as smart as Harrods, and the exterior facade —a half-timbered mock-Tudor palace—is the most distinctive in London. Liberty's basement is home to china, glass and the "Pots, Pans and Rags" department—the highest-styled of these types in town. The main floor is largely men's—the celebrated Liberty print ties—mostly paisley designs in fine silk, but also in equally fine cotton. Up a flight, on one, is one of the best men's clothing departments in town—suits, sport jackets, sweaters and turtle-necks, and—not to be overlooked—Liberty's superfine cottons in a variety of designs, made up into collarless dressing gowns that are perfect traveling companions. The second floor features the firm's fine silks and cottons, sold by the yard as well a note-worthy women's and children's clothing departments. Higher up are furniture and a small restaurant (Chapter 5).

Dickins & Jones is Liberty's next-door Regent Street neighbor. It is a medium-size, medium-category store, specializing mainly in women's clothing, but with a compact main-floor men's cloth-ing department and a top-floor restaurant (Chapter 5).

Swan & Edgar (Regent Street at Piccadilly Circus) is smack in the heart of tourist territory, with its own entrance to the Pic-cadilly Circus Underground station. The emphasis is on moderate-category merchandise. The main floor has a convenient souvenir shop, with some not-bad gifts among quantities of the usual embarrassments. The rest of the floor is largely women's ac-cessories—scarves and the like, as well as cosmetics and per-fumes. More women's clothing is upstairs on one and two. Higher up—on four—one finds luggage, and an uncommonly good book department, with considerable easy-to-fly-with paperbacks availa-ble. This same floor is home to china—including a big Wedgwood section. Restaurants (Chapter 5) are on five and in the basement, which is largely devoted to a rather extensive men's clothing de-partment and from which one enters the Underground.

Fortnum & Mason (Piccadilly) extends from that principal thor-oughfare through to fashionable Jermyn Street. It is one of London's loveliest stores, and understandably a favorite with visitors, most especially Americans. The trademark on the main floor—which is largely given over to the firm's famous food de-partments—is the corps of tail-coated salesmen. Many customers never get beyond this floor. Here are all of Fortnum's own-make fancy groceries—teas in great variety, brown sugar crystals of the kind often seen in English sugar bowls, exotic coffee blends, jams galore, fruit-and-delicacy baskets of especial splendor, a tempting *charcuterie*-delicatessen section with cheeses in profusion (domestics like Wensleydale, Cheshire and Stilton, but imports too), a bakery with the elaborate cakes that the English call by the French name, *gâteaux,* superlative produce and wine departments, and the celebrated Fortnum's Fountain (Chapter 5).

Fortnum's basement is home to choice selections of china, glass, luggage, leather and silver. The first floor (up a flight from main) is devoted to women's clothes and accessories—expensive, essentially conservative, but attractive; there's a women's hairdresser here, too. The second floor is a delight: toys for the kids and clothes for them as well. Men's clothes and accessories (a cashmere sweater from here is a long-possessed treasure of mine) are on three, along with a men's barber shop, appliances and gifts. The fourth floor shares antiques with a restaurant. (Eating at Fortnum's is dealt with in Chapter 5).

Harvey Nichols (Knightsbridge, just opposite the Hyde Park Hotel in Knightsbridge) is Harrods' major neighbor and is in the same expensive range, concentrating on quality women's wear and accessories. Additionally, one finds departments devoted to antiques, contemporary furniture, fabrics by the yard, china and glassware. There is, as well, a main-floor men's shop that is a branch of Jaeger. The basement café is oddly unappealing.

Peter Jones (Sloane Square) occupies such an architecturally striking pre-World War II building—it is considered among the better contemporary London structures—that one is disappointed once inside. Chelsea deserves a far more modish department store. The more interesting departments are china, glass and gifts on main, luggage on two, and toys on three. (The fourth-floor restaurants are described in Chapter 5.)

Barkers (Kensington High Street) is an enterprise worth one's acquaintance—an old-timer that stays with the times, but remains recognizable as a reliable family department store. The high-ceilinged main floor contains an appetizing food hall, with adjacent candy and flower shops and—worth knowing, this—a pharmacy. Women's accessories, cosmetics and souvenirs—including a big selection of dish towels with London designs—are also on main. The clothing departments—there's a big one for men, and many for women and children—are on the upper floors, with a good china, glass and gift section on five, next to the pleasant restaurant that is described in Chapter 5.

The Army & Navy Stores (Victoria Street) is a nice old-fashioned department store near Victoria Station with which you may want to become acquainted. The title—going back to a time when military officers and their families in the colonies were among the chief customers—is a misnomer, for the store's wares are not unlike those of the competition. Main-floor groceries, wines, cosmetics, and women's accessories; and a wide range of departments including china and glass, hardware (gardening equipment is a noted specialty) and housewares, men's and women's clothing and accessories.

STREET MARKETS

London's street markets may not yield what you are looking for, as regards purchases. But they are peculiar to London, an intrinsic part of the city's mercantile scene, and a lot of fun to explore, in the bargain.

Petticoat Lane (Middlesex Street) is the most amusing. It's a Sunday morning proposition, with the prime hours between 9 A.M. and noon. There are hundreds of stalls lining Middlesex and adjacent streets, and they defy easy classification. One chap is selling shopping bags full of six or seven boxes full of delicious-looking chocolates (heaven knows where he got them) for a pittance . . . another vends clocks, watches and jewelry. There are stalls with the traditional whelks and cockles and mussels of old London . . . stands with Indian shirts and saris and sandals . . . quantities of luggage, most of it cheap plastic, but not all . . . demonstrations in lovely-to-listen-to Cockney, of vegetable slicers and innumerable other gadgets . . . china and kitchenware . . . blue jeans and dress suits . . . linens and towels. And interspersed among the good-natured crowds are sandwich boards attached to grim-visaged elderly men, with anything but optimistic intelligence. The advice is to the effect that "The End Is At Hand" and readers of the boards are, as a consequence asked to "Flee From the Wrath to Come."

The Portobello Road Market (Portobello Road) is another visitor favorite. This is really two different kinds of market. On early-morning weekdays the wares are flowers, fruit and vegetables. The more interesting market is Saturdays only (usually from about 8:30 A.M. until 6 P.M.) when antiques are the specialty. One should qualify that: *some* antiques, interspersed among quantities of merely elderly objects, some of which are at least amusing. But have a look for yourself.

The Camden Passage Antiques Market (Camden Passage) is situated in Islington, an old London neighborhood that has become fashionable in recent years. You are a good bus or taxi ride from the center of town, but the trip is worthwhile for there are the wares of something like a hundred shops. Hours are 10:30 A.M.– 5:30 P.M. Mondays through Saturdays, with the alfresco stalls open only on Monday, Wednesday and Saturdays.

The New Caledonian Antiques Market (Bermondsey Square) is an old-fashioned open-air affair with more than 250 vendors of antiques, bibelots and what-have-you. Fridays only, from 7 A.M. until 3 P.M.

Shepherd Market (between Curzon Street and Piccadilly) is a two-centuries-old sector of Mayfair that is a maze of small shops, vegetable stalls, restaurants, pubs and cafés. Each enterprise keeps its own hours. The market area makes for pleasurable ambles.

ANTIQUES

There are still considerable quantities of English seventeenth-, eighteenth-, and nineteenth-century furniture, ceramics, porcelain, books, maps, paintings, clocks, tapestries and other objects

available in London, not to mention antiques of other areas—
France, Italy, the Middle East, the Orient—which cost more.
One can buy at the big noted dealers and auction houses but
also to be considered are smaller places—often with good prices
—on Knightsbridge's Brompton Road, Chelsea's King's Road,
Kensington's Fulham Road and Church Street, and the Portobello Road.

To be noted also is the big and annual high-caliber Antiques
Fair held for a fortnight in mid-June at Grosvenor House Hotel.
Here, alphabetically, are some sources:

Antiquarius (133 King's Road): A maze of individual dealers,
each in his own stall, with nary a dull-looking display in the lot,
which includes old prints, jewelry, books, silver, china and heaven
knows what all else. Fun to look at, even for non-buyers.

The Antique Porcelain Co., Ltd. (149 New Bond Street): Eighteenth-century porcelain.

Arthur Davidson (178 New Bond Street): Mostly seventeenth-
century furniture.

Asprey & Co., Ltd. (165 New Bond Street): Antiques are only
a department of this jewelry-silver-leather-watch-gift shop. But
what antiques! They are one flight up, they are all described
and priced on extra-complete labels, and they are invariably
museum caliber.

Aubrey Brocklehurst (124 Cromwell Road): English clocks,
watches and barometers.

Bernard Quartich (5 Lower John Street): Old and rare books.

Bond Street Silver Galleries (111 New Bond Street): Old silver.

Dark & Rendlesham (498 King's Road): English furniture from
Elizabeth I through the seventeenth century.

Frank Partridge (144 New Bond Street): No better source for
English and French furniture; with a New York branch.

H. Blairman & Sons (36 New Bond Street): Regency and other nineteenth-century English furniture and paintings.

Holmes & Co. (New Bond Street): Eighteenth-century silver, Victorian jewelry, plate from the nineteen-twenties and thirties.

Hypermarket (26–40 Kensington High Street): A hundred dealers, each with his own stall; all guarantee refunds if fakes—perish the thought—are unintentionally sold to customers.

J. and J. May (40 Kensington Church Street): Furniture, at mostly moderate prices.

John Reid (42 Kensington Church Street): Fine old bird-prints.

London Silver Vaults (Chancery Lane): Old silver and china; experts at shipping.

Mallett & Son (40 New Bond Street and 2 Davies Street): Nothing less than the fanciest antiquary in the kingdom, with both domestic and French wares. The Davies Street shop, to give you an idea, is the one-time home of the Duke of Westminster.

Ning (8 Symans Street): Charming offbeat pieces—early Victorian wicker, for example, or stripped-pine country pieces. Behind Peter Jones department store.

Oliver Sutton (34-C Kensington Church Street): Victorian Staffordshire figures.

Phillips & Harris (54 Kensington Church Street): Mostly nineteenth-century things—furniture and objects as well.

Stair & Co. (Mount Street): This firm—near the Connaught Hotel—is one of the leaders, with first-quality furniture, both English and imported, and other objects as well.

Tessier (26 New Bond Street): Exceptional antique gold, silver, vermeilware and jewelry.

Tilley & Co. (2 Symons Street): Unusual porcelain and pewter-ware, sixteenth through nineteenth centuries; behind Peter Jones department store in Chelsea.

Vita Juel (99–101 Kensington Church Street): Superlative Chinese porcelain.

ANTIQUES AUCTION HOUSES

There are half a dozen-odd major auction houses. Most advertise in *The Daily Telegraph* in advance of their sales of all manner of old things—furniture, paintings, porcelain, old books and maps, silver, rugs and carpets, and imported objects from Chinese ceramics to Italian majolica. Generally, the sources of the merchandise are stated; these are usually from estates of collectors. Contents of each sale are on view in the auction rooms two days before the auctioneer bangs his gavel. Often, there are catalogues of the merchandise, obtainable in advance by mail and at advertised prices. The firms include:

Bonhams (Montpelier Street, in Knightsbridge).

Christie, Manson & Woods (8 King Street): Known locally simply as Christie's, and with a New York branch.

Sotheby & Co. (34–35 New Bond Street) is affiliated with Parke, Bernet in New York. It has a Belgravia outpost, running its own auctions, at 19 Montcomb Street.

ART GALLERIES

Galleries are concentrated in and about South Kensington, Bond Street and the St. James's area. An interesting group:

Andrew Block (20 Barter Street) makes a specialty of antique London playbills and old prints.

Color Print Gallery (2 Montcomb Street) sells lithographs by modern greats, some quite reasonably.

Fine Art Society (148 New Bond Street) is big on English water colors, old ones at that, and fairly priced.

Kasmin Gallery (118 New Bond Street) is for trendy British work —where it's at this very week.

Arthur Tooth & Sons (31 Bruton Street) is an old-reliable for works of this and the last centuries; Continental (with Impressionist emphasis) but British, as well.

Weinreb & Douwma (92 Great Russell Street) is a treasure-trove of lovely old prints and maps, heavily English in origin.

Wildenstein (147 New Bond Street): Museum-caliber paintings, antique and otherwise; also in New York and Paris.

BARBERS AND HAIRDRESSERS

No need to anticipate a poor haircut or hairset in this of all cities. The British are expert barbers and hairdressers. Here are a few recommended places:

Barbers:

The Crimpers (80a Baker Street): Unisex, youngish, modish.

Fortnum & Mason (Piccadilly): Adjacent to the men's clothing department; tends to veer toward the conservative.

Harrods (Knightsbridge): The shop is called The Trimmers and it's in that offbeat, mod part of the store called Way In, on the fourth floor. Very contemporary.

Ivan (20 Jermyn Street): A big shop, with barbers on two levels, generally cutting hair expertly and—if you specify—the way you want it.

George F. Trumper (Curzon Street): The greatest old-fashioned barber shop of them all. But old-fashioned does not necessarily mean square; count on a good haircut.

Hairdressers:

The Crimpers (80a Baker Street): Unisex, mod.

Elizabeth Arden (20 New Bond Street): The old reliable, red door and all.

Fortnum & Mason (Piccadilly): Establishment-safe.

Harrods (Knightsbridge): A big shop with a diverse staff; invariably satisfactory.

Leonard's (6 Upper Grosvenor Street): Top models like its high-style trademark.

BOOKSHOPS

Books published in Britain are no longer the bargains they used to be, but they are still good buys, and the output of the publishers is prodigious, both hard-bound and paperback. The industry has more than its share of top-rank typographic designers and printers, so that most books are very handsome to look upon. Here are a handful of the more interesting shops. Most will ship—worth noting as the book rate (by sea, of course) is very cheap.

Collet's Bookstore (64 Charing Cross Road): A general selection, from all publishers.

Collet's Penguin Bookshop (52 Charing Cross Road): A near-neighbor of the shop above, with the specialty Penguin paperbacks, in glorious profusion.

John Faustus (94 Jermyn Street): Old and rare books—beauties—are the specialty.

Foyles (119 Charing Cross Road): An oldie, occupying considerable space, and with books on the most unlikely specialized subjects. Allow some time if you are easily addicted to prolonged browsing. Expert at shipping.

Hatchards (187 Piccadilly): In business since the end of the eighteenth century. Virtually all of the new books; fiction and otherwise. Paperbacks in abundance, and if they don't have it, they'll order it for you. There is a special department devoted to Antiquarian Books (in a special room on the second floor), and its personnel will search for out-of-print volumes for you if they're not in stock. There is, as well, a bookbinding service—full or half-leather bindings on any books you select. Hatchards are very big on catalogues on special subjects—garden books, for example. They'll put you on their mailing list, for any or all of their catalogues, and they ship well.

Her Majesty's Stationery Office (49 High Holborn and 423 Oxford Street) sells the low-priced but frequently fascinating publications published by the government on a wide range of subjects.

John Menzies (Strand) is big, modern, well-stocked with current titles, both cloth and paper, as well as periodicals.

Selfridges (Oxford Street) has a super main-floor book department that is very big on paperbacks (you may *think* you own every mystery Agatha Christie or Ngaio Marsh has written, but you had better check the stocks here). And this department store's magazine-newspaper stall is quite possibly the best—and most complete—in town.

W. H. Smith & Son is everywhere throughout the kingdom, selling books, magazines, newspapers and stationery. One of their most impressive stores is a modern self-service one—selling all of the above—on Sloane Square in Chelsea.

Zwemmer (Charing Cross Road) makes a specialty of art books, and I'll be surprised if they don't have what you're looking for.

CHILDREN'S CLOTHES AND TOYS

The earlier recommended department stores are excellent for children's clothes and toys—Harrods, Selfridges, Fortnum & Mason especially. But here are some additional sources:

Marks & Spencer (173 and 485 Oxford Street) is a nationwide cheap-clothing chain that purports to sell nearly 11 per cent of all the clothing purveyed in the United Kingdom. You don't always find what you want, but you just may, especially in the children's departments.

N. Peal (37–40 Burlington Arcade) has handsome children's clothes and accessories—in cashmere, other wools, and linen. Women's things, too.

Pollocks (44 Monmouth Street) is a spectacular toyland.

Rowes (120 New Bond Street) has very smart, high-style kids' clothes. Expensive.

Small Wonder (296 King's Road) specializes in togs and toys for youngsters up to six.

CHINA AND POTTERY

The department stores excel in this category—Harrods and Liberty are exceptional, and Selfridges has a good department. But there are additional important sources, some of which follow.

Chinacraft Ltd. (499 Oxford Street, 50 Brompton Road, 71 Regent Street) has absolutely enormous selections of such makes as Royal Doulton, Royal Crown Derby, Minton, Wedgwood and Royal Worcester. Big names in crystal too, including Ireland's Waterford. And shipping is a specialty.

Gered of London (173–74 Piccadilly and 134 Regent Street) specializes in Spode and Wedgwood, with an astonishing variety of lovely patterns. They ship expertly, too.

The Reject China Shop (33–34 and 42 Beauchamp Place) occupies two separate shops, each of which is chock full of seconds—some you'll like, some not. There is bone china and pottery as well, from a number of manufacturers. And there are always a lot of lookers.

CHOCOLATES

Bendicks Mayfair Ltd. (New Bond Street at Maddox Street) makes wickedly delicious chocolates and packs them beautifully in containers ranging from cardboard to Wedgwood. Expensive.

Charbonnel et Walker (31 Old Bond Street) is an elegant chocolatier. Each chocolate is numbered, if you please. And the boxes are as handsome as the chocolates are irresistible. Expensive.

Richoux (86 Brompton Road) vends its own esteemed chocolates and doubles as a highly caloric morning-coffee-lunch-afternoon-tearoom. Expensive.

DOODADS

Herbert Johnson (38 New Bond Street) is surely the most off-beat merchant to ever hold a royal warrant. His line of miscellany includes women's floppy cotton hats, men's ties, straw boaters, pillboxes and pincushions such as you've never seen before, funny suspenders, amusing kerchiefs—and I don't know what all else. Everything has style and panache.

Halcyon Days, Ltd. (14 Brook Street) is a tiny Mayfair shop whose specialties are reproductions of the little Battersea boxes of old. There are other small enamel-on-copper objects, too—all of them charming copies of the eighteenth-century originals.

DUTY-FREE SHOPPING

Heathrow Airport (Heathrow): The duty-free shops at Heathrow sell wide varieties of Scotch, English gin, and other spirits and liqueurs; French perfumes and colognes; cigarettes; Swiss watches and clocks; Japanese cameras and radios; electric shavers from several countries; and British products including Pringle and Braemar cashmere, Liberty scarves and Wedgwood china.

KITCHEN EQUIPMENT

The department stores shine in this area; Liberty, Selfridges and Harrods are particularly strong. But here are a few additional sources.

David Mellor, Ironmonger (4 Sloane Square) sells hardware on the main floor of his uncommonly well-designed shop, and housewares and kitchen equipment in the basement. The place is full of reasonably tabbed cooking implements, baskets, cutlery, pottery and glassware.

Elizabeth David (46 Bourne Street) is a gifted writer of cookbooks —her work was a major stimulus behind England's post-World War II interest in Mediterranean foods. And her shop is full of the equipment she considers essential for a good kitchen.

The Reject Shop (Brompton Road) is full of seconds of smartly styled kitchen equipment and housewares, at good prices.

FABRICS BY THE YARD

Clothing fabrics—assuming you have someone at home to make them up for you, whose labor is not so costly that it will make the total cost exorbitant—can be good buys in London. Here are two good sources:

Liberty (Regent Street) is celebrated for its fine silks and cottons; it makes these up into articles of clothings, of course, from neckties to dresses. But it sells by the yard, too.

The Scotch House (2 Brompton Road and 84 Regent Street) is an Edinburgh firm with the largest selection of tartans extant, and a great deal else of beauty and quality. Of its two London stores, I prefer the Brompton Road one, in Knightsbridge.

HANDICRAFTS

Handicrafts are not the sort of thing one expects in as industrialized a country as Britain, but there are exceptional selections in London at these two sources:

The Commonwealth Crafts Centre (35 Victoria Street) sells unusual handicrafts from artisans living in Commonwealth countries around the world.

The Crafts Council Gallery (12 Waterloo Place) retails the work of British craftsmen.

JEWELRY

Asprey & Co., Ltd. (165–69 New Bond Street) is earlier recommended for its antiques. But it is even more celebrated as a source of fine jewels, watches, and silver; gifts, too. Very old, very reliable.

S. J. Phillips (113 New Bond Street) makes a specialty of lovely antique jewelry—Georgian through Victorian.

KNITWEAR AND SWEATERS

Knitwear and sweaters are nowhere finer than those of the United Kingdom, where they remain a bit cheaper than when purchased in the United States. There are good sources everywhere. Here are a handful:

Harrods (Knightsbridge) sells fine-quality knit sweaters and the like in the Men's Store, and women's knits at departments throughout the store.

Jaeger (204 Regent Street) has smart, expensive knitwear for both men and women.

Lilleywhites (Piccadilly Circus) has a big knitwear department for women on its first floor and sells men's knitwear in the various men's departments.

Marks & Spencer (173 and 458 Oxford Street) is big on knitwear for the family—Mom, Dad and the kids. Inexpensive.

The Scotch House (2 Brompton Road and 84 Regent Street) has a tremendous selection of cashmeres, Shetlands and other woolens for both sexes.

Selfridges (Oxford Street) has men's sweaters and turtlenecks, scarves and wool shirts in its men's accessory department on the main floor; and women's knitwear in its women's departments.

S. Fisher (108 Piccadilly and Burlington Arcade, Shop Nos. 42–43) specializes in cashmere and Shetland sweaters for men and women, and Allen Solly lisle shirts for men. His prices are good.

LEATHER

Leather is of exceptional quality in England; the findings and catches on bags, wallets, luggage and briefcases are often superior to those on the Continent, and the quality of the skins and of the tanning is invariably good. There are many first-rate sources.

Gidden's of London (74 New Oxford Street and 153 Clifford Street) is a venerable firm which is at once a saddlery and a general leather-goods house. Equestrians will want to know it for its riding equipment, but other leather-goods buyers will find it of interest too. It makes and retails its own saddle soap.

Harrods (Knightsbridge) has a leather department that is unsurpassed in London—briefcases, handbags, luggage, wallets, the works. Excellent style and quality.

Loewe (25 Old Bond Street) is not British, but rather a branch of the noted Madrid leather house. The stuff is beautiful, albeit expensive—women's handbags, briefcases, wallets, luggage.

Unicorn Leather (Burlington Arcade, Shop No. 41) sells handsome bags and briefcases, and will custom-make whatever it is you may have in mind.

PERFUMES, SOAPS AND COLOGNES

Perfumes, soaps and colognes—the last two for men as well as women—make welcome gifts from Britain, at least if they are English-made. Here are some suggestions.

Floris (89 Jermyn Street) has been making its own soaps, colognes and perfumes since the early eighteenth century, when the business was started by a Señor Floris out of the Spanish island of Minorca; the fifth generation of the family carries on. The women's perfumes embrace nearly a dozen English-flower scents —from English Violet to Stephanotis. There are toilet waters in even more scents, sachets, face creams, even a mouthwash with a rose-perfume base. Floris soaps are celebrated. So are the pomanders. And the men's line—No. 89—for the street number of the shop—is best known for the lime toilet water. But there is a much cheaper after-shave, as well as talc, hair lotion, shaving cream and soap, and toilet soap.

George F. Trumper (9 Curzon Street) is an ancient institution. It does two things: cuts men's hair and puts up men's lime after-shave in wonderful bottles with lead stoppers in the form of crowns. Of late the lime has been supplemented by other scents. But I stick with the old original. Trumper ships, and expertly.

Savory & Moore Ltd. (143 New Bond Street) is about as posh a pharmacy as you'll come across in London. Soaps, colognes and perfumes are a specialty, especially the line made by Taylor of London, with products for both men and women. Savory & Moore put out their own bath cologne—it makes an excellent after-shave for men as well—in a plastic bottle. It's inexpensive and English, and if you ask them to gift-wrap it for you (they do this beautifully), you have a handsome gift.

Yardley (New Bond Street, at Stafford Street) sells the whole Yardley line—perfumes, colognes, soaps, after-shaves, shaving cream, the works—from this attractive shop in the home town.

STATIONERY

Stationery is nowhere smarter than in England—plain, printed or engraved, with name and address or simply with monogram.

Frank Smythson, Ltd. (54 New Bond Street) is unsurpassed among stationers. They make a specialty of pale blue paper, engraved in a darker blue. But their range is vast, from pristine white to shocking pink, with styles for both men and women.

They will, of course, ship your order to you (engraving takes time) if it's not ready when you leave town; and, if you like, they'll keep the die—or plate—so that you can reorder by mail.

UMBRELLAS

It goes without saying: Umbrellas are best when English. No other people, unhappily, has more experience using them. Still, it is said of the derby-topped chaps who work in the City that they would rather be drenched than unfurl their impeccably rolled brollies. Well no matter.

Swain, Adeney Briggs & Sons (185 Piccadilly) is a noted source, not only of umbrellas, but of walking sticks as well.

MEN'S CLOTHES, ACCESSORIES AND SHOES

If there is any truth in the old bromide that "London is a man's town" it is because no city in the world offers gents a greater selection of clothes. There is no question but that British tailoring leads the world. Until not too many years ago, the problem was with styling, which was considerably behind contemporary trends in the Western world. But that has long since changed. London clothiers, tailors, haberdashers, hatters, shoe sellers—the lot— cater not only to the British equivalent of the American Brooks Brothers arch-conservative, but also to the way-out mod man, and to the great majority of us in the middle, as well. Here is a selected group of sources that I find interesting. They are presented alphabetically by firm name.

Aquascutum (100 Regent Street) is known on both sides of the Atlantic. Its line is smart and bold but never aggressively so. Raincoats are a specialty, but there are suits, sports jackets and interesting accessories, especially neckties. A more mod group of clothes is sold in the store's ground floor Club 92. There's a women's shop too. Expensive.

Austin Reed (on both Regent Street and Knightsbridge) is moderate-to-expensive, attractively middle-of-the-road in its styling. The quality is good, and the line is complete—suits, jackets, slacks, coats, and accessories.

Bugati (59 Kensington Church Street) is smallish, smartish, and moderate-to-expensive, with good-looking suits, jackets, and coats, not to mention shirts, ties and sweaters that make super presents.

Burberrys (18–22 Haymarket) is another old-timer that stays happily but not aggressively youthful. This firm's raincoats and overcoats are legendary (Burberry selects some of the handsomest tweeds in town for the latter). The sportswear is handsome; so are accessories, including well-priced wool plaid ties. A recent addition is luggage, canvas with the plaid the very same that is traditional in the lining of Burberry raincoats. Moderate to expensive.

Casidy (114–116 King's Road) is a vendor of shirts, jackets and suits, at happily moderate prices.

Codner, Coombs & Dobbie (21 Jermyn Street) is a celebrated men's shoe shop, exemplifying British shoemaking at its best.

The Common Market (121 King's Road) is one of a number of shops in the King's Road area specializing in blue jeans, and appropriate accessories.

Dolci's (Knightsbridge and at locations all over town) sells good-looking men's shoes at low prices. (Women's, too.)

Geezer's (38 Kensington Church Street) is for young-look suits in the low-price category.

Harrods (Knightsbridge) has in its Men's Shop one of London's leading sources of quality, relatively conservative clothing and accessories. The same store's Way In shop is quite the reverse as regards styling—mod and bold. And with more moderate prices.

Hawes & Curtis (2 Burlington Gardens) is a long-time creator of custom shirts, than which there is nothing more luxurious.

Henry Maxwell (9 Dover Street) is a noted maker of custom shoes; expensive, but luxuriant. If they're not ready before you leave for home, they'll be shipped.

Jaeger's (204–206 Regent Street) line—suits, jackets, coats, all manner of accessories including handsome ties—is expensive and stylish, even if its salesmen are not the most congenial in London.

John Michael (18 Savile Row and Jermyn Street near Bury Street) has a remarkably high level of taste in its clothes and accessories. The prices are moderate to high, and the sweaters, shirts and ties make excellent gifts. The bigger Savile Row store—sleek chrome and black—is one of London's most strikingly good-looking commercial interiors. Courteous salespeople.

Liberty (Regent Street) is one of the best of London sources for neckties (both silk and cotton Liberty prints—mostly paisley-type designs); three-quarter-length, three-quarter-sleeve bathrobes (in fine Liberty cotton); sweaters (there is an enormous Shetland selection); suits and coats. And the staff is helpful and efficient.

Lilleywhites (Piccadilly Circus) is a five-story monument to sportswear—golf, tennis, ski togs and sports equipment, as well; and for women as well as men. There is, in addition, a modish men's clothing department, with Chester Barrie suits and a wide choice of suede jackets and knitwear.

Lock's (6 St. James's Street) is a venerable hatter, for a bowler (what we call a derby), a trilby or just an everyday felt hat or wool cap: Lock's has them all.

Lord John (72 King's Road) is a big shop with a good-looking line of moderate-priced men's clothing and accessories; women's department upstairs.

Lotus (43 New Bond Street) is for casual, heavy-duty walking, wet-weather and hard-work shoes and boots; there's a women's department too.

Marks & Spencer (173 and 458 Oxford Street) is a nationwide cheap-clothing chain that purports to supply Britain with 11 per cent of the clothing it wears. Its secret is good value for little money. Which does not necessarily mean style or fine quality. But you never know what you might find; worth a look around in the course of an Oxford Street shopping expedition. There is a full line of clothing and accessories; sweaters and raincoats are often among the better buys.

Mates (82 King's Road) sells young-in-spirit clothing, at young prices.

Michael Barrie (Oxford Street near Duke Street) has high-style, albeit low-priced, clothing and accessories.

Pierre Cardin (Strand at Trafalgar Square) has Cardin suits and blazers at prices well under those for Cardin clothes in France or the United States.

Russell & Bromley (Brompton Road) has smartly designed shoes for men, and for that matter for women too. Moderate.

Savile Row—a selection of bespoke (custom) tailors:

> **Hawkes,** at No. 1, is perhaps the most commercial-minded of the lot. It is very big, very old, and very respectable, but also very square and unexciting, with a ready-made line as well as bespoke.

> **Nutters,** at 35a, is young in spirit, staff and styling; takes three weeks to make a suit, has high tabs, but appears conscientious.

> **Taylor-Coulson's** (No. 16): Mr. Goldie is a Scot at once charming and canny, with a policy of five working days to complete;

a good line of good fabrics; sensible, realistic prices; and an extensive American (and otherwise foreign) clientele.

Tobias Brothers Ltd. (No. 32) is conservative, expensive, and takes its time.

Vincent's (No. 10) will make up a suit in as little as five days. Attractive materials. Expensive.

The Scotch House (2 Brompton Road and 84 Regent Street) has the largest collection of tartans extant—some 300 of them beautifully displayed in a Tartan Hall, if that it may be called. You may get them made up into a number of things. Additionally, there is an extensive men's department. Lots of Scottish cashmeres and Shetlands are on hand.

Simpson (Piccadilly) is an always-reliable men's store, neither conservative nor bold, with both clothing and accessories. At least in most of the store. The interesting exception is the Trend Shop, which while hardly mod is headed in that direction. Additionally: barber shop, theater-ticket bureau and slow-service restaurant, as well as a women's department. Simpson distributes a handy (and gratis) map of central London, with theaters and cinemas designated.

Stanley Adams (Kensington High Street) sells cheap, albeit good looking, contemporary-style suits.

Take Six (Kensington Church Street, 59 King's Road, and 91 New Bond Street at Oxford Street) is among the leaders in the low-priced, albeit stylish, men's clothing revolution. If the salesmen are not always courteous, the suits are handsome, made of good-looking materials, and cheap.

Turnbull & Asser (71 Jermyn Street and around the corner on Bury Street) is an aged institution that went mod a few years back, losing some of its politesse in the process, but emerging with handsome though expensive, four-in-hand and extra-wide bow ties. The staff remains snippy at the Jermyn Street shop, but for some reason or other the branch shop, just around the corner on Bury Street (with its own entrance), has as kind and helpful a crew as one could ask.

The Village Gate (Regent Street and 131 King's Road) sells super-looking clothes and accessories, at sensible prices.

WOMEN'S CLOTHES, ACCESSORIES AND SHOES

Biba (Kensington High Street) is an Art Deco palace, with Art Deco salesladies selling Art Deco clothes, shoes, accessories, doo-dads and what have you—at high prices. There are some men's things too, and newer departments carrying kids' togs, flowers, magazines, and—in the basement—an amusing food section. Go to have a look even if you don't buy a thing, not missing the fountain-accented, two-acre roof garden. The setting is the one-time Derry & Toms department store, all re-done in camp Thirties' style—even including a peach-marble-floored restaurant. Fun.

BoPeep (37 Kensington High Street) is amusing, stylish and moderately priced.

Bus Stop (3 Kensington Church Street) is very contemporary. Middling prices.

Che Guevara (44 Kensington High Street) has clothes quite as disarming as its name—which is to say, very interesting. The decor is Art Deco.

Chelsea Cobbler (165 Draycott Avenue) makes women's shoes to order; expensive but of high quality and workmanship, with you yourself having a say in the styling if you like.

Cresta (148 Sloane Street) has silk and print dresses neither bold nor conservative: the essence of good English taste. Moderate to expensive.

Crocodile (98 New Bond Street) specializes in very smart but not very way-out clothes. Costly.

Dolci's (Knightsbridge and at many other locations) specializes in stylish shoes at low prices. Men's as well as women's.

Elle (92 New Bond Street at Oxford Street) has very good clothes with very good style. Moderate to expensive.

Fenwick (New Bond Street, corner of Brook Street) is a multi-story women's specialty shop with stylish clothes and accessories at mostly moderate prices. Worth noting here are the restaurant and cafeteria (Chapter 5) with a fancy grocery too.

Hardy Amies (14 Savile Row, in a house which had been inhabited by Richard Brinsley Sheridan) is one of England's pre-eminent couturiers. Expensive.

Harrods (Knightsbridge) is as great a women's clothing store as it is a great department store. One has only to case its Knightsbridge women's windows, let alone its various women's clothing and accessories departments, to appreciate its unerring style. The range is from conservative to trendy, with most in between, and the mod in the remarkable Way In shop, verily a store within a store.

Harvey Nichols (Knightsbridge) is a neighbor of Harrods, with several floors full of moderate to expensive clothes and accessories.

Jaeger (204–206 Regent Street) emphasizes smart, understated and expensive sport clothes.

James Drew (Shop No. 3, Burlington Arcade, Piccadilly) specializes in separates for women, in knits and woolens; good looking, moderate to expensive.

Kurt Geiger (New Bond Street at Blenheim, near Oxford Street) sells high-style shoes, mostly Italian. Attractive and expensive.

Le Bistro (93 King's Road) is a trendy boutique, moderate priced.

Marisa Martin (46 Brompton Road) has novel, original clothes: peasant, twenties, thirties; moderate-priced.

Mary Durant (137 Sloane Street) specializes in clothes that are at once modish but subdued—in good taste. Moderate to expensive, and across the street from earlier-recommended Cresta.

Miss Selfridge at Selfridges (Oxford Street) is a mammoth store within a store; the emphasis is stylish fashion for young-minded customers, at young prices. A London success story.

Norman Hartnell (26 Bruton Street) is the Queen's dressmaker. Expensive.

Stirling Cooper (New Bond Street, corner of Blenheim and near Oxford) sells way-out women's clothes and accessories—innovative, bold, and of good quality and taste; moderate prices. There's a back-of-shop men's department in a similar vein, with mod music in the background.

Tyger (35 Kensington Church Street) is, not unsurprisingly—given that name—a source of aggressively styled clothes and accessories, with a young look. Middle-priced.

7 *London:* *To Note*

ACCESS

More *airlines* fly from the United States to London than to any other European capital. These include British Airways (BOAC), National Airlines, Trans World Airlines (TWA), Pan American World Airways, Air-India, and British Caledonian.

British lines link London and the capitals of Europe, whose countries' own carriers provide additional extensive air service. There is, as well, considerable domestic air service within the British Isles.

London Airport, at Heathrow, is fourteen miles from town, making taxis a fairly expensive proposition; the airport buses to the several London air terminals, run frequently, and are cheap and efficient; taxis are readily available at the air terminals in town, to take passengers to hotels. Still another airport, *Gatwick,* is more distant from the city; of the transatlantic carriers, only British Caledonian uses it.

There are a number of *air terminals* in London; each airline is assigned one. They include *Buckingham Palace Road,* used by British Airways and other major airlines; *West London,* used by British and many Continental airlines for flights between London and the Continent; *Kensington High Street,* used by a number of lines including TWA; *Victoria Station,* used by Icelandic and British Caledonian, and *Brompton Road,* used principally by Aer Lingus-Irish.

There is excellent *train service* between London and the Continental capitals and Ireland, thanks to trains co-ordinating with ship sailings across the North and Irish seas and the English Channel. British Transport's domestic rail services are good—and sometimes excellent; there are crack luxury expresses to Edinburgh and other major cities, and one does well to consider sightseeing excursions—as short as a day's duration—to innumerable British points by train.

London has more than a dozen *railway stations*—surely it sets a world record among cities, in this respect—so that it is essential to clearly understand from where one will depart on trains. Of this large group of terminals, the more important to be familiar with are *King's Cross* (trains to the north, through to Edinburgh), *Euston* (trains to the north, through to Glasgow, and boat trains to Ireland, via Liverpool), *Charing Cross* (with trains mainly for the southeast), *Liverpool Street* (trainings heading east), *Paddington* (for west and southwest points), *Waterloo* (south) and *Victoria* (southern points and the Continent).

The traveler who plans on fairly intensive travel within Britain does well to consider purchasing the bargain-priced *BritRail Pass* —the UK's counterpart of the Continent's Eurailpass—from travel agents or BritRail Travel International's U.S. office at 270 Madison Avenue, New York, New York 10016. Note that the pass must be purchased in North America, in advance of one's arrival in the UK—where it is *not* available. There are both first-class and economy-class passes, each good for unlimited travel for periods of 8 days, 15 days, 21 days and a month, with the fares (subject to change) ranging from $40 (8-day economy) to $115 (one-month first class). If you are on a budget, my advice is to select economy class.

The British Rail Travel Centre (12 Lower Regent Street) is a mine of information on all phases of rail travel, both domestic and international, and it has gratis brochures on British Transport's package tours of Britain and on their rail-sea journeys to the Continent.

GETTING ABOUT IN LONDON

Public transport is excellent. The subway—officially the *Underground* but also known as the *Tube*—is one of the best such systems in the world; free route maps of the system are available from the ticket-sellers at every station, and I suggest you procure one without delay because you will want to take full advantage of the Underground. It is fast, cheap, clean, safe, and without the graffiti that is a temporary phenomenon on systems in cities like New York. The Underground embraces eight major lines, each of whose routes has a color of its own on the system maps. Ascertain the Underground station nearest to your destination, determine which line it is on, and plot your route by means of the system map, noting whatever transfers en route may be necessary. The stations indicated by big circles on the map as "Interchanges" are where you may transfer to connecting lines. There is only one class of travel, unlike the two in Paris, and fares are determined by the length of one's trip. You announce your destination to the ticket agent when purchasing your ticket, and he'll tell you the amount of your fare. Remember to hold on to your ticket for surrender at journey's end. And remember, too, that Underground ticket agents and conductors are invariably helpful. If at all in doubt about your trip—particularly if you will have transfers to make en route—don't hesitate to ask for help.

London *buses* can be a more complicated matter. But the stops on each route are clearly listed at each and every bus-halt. By studying these and sampling them, you soon become aware as to which of the bus routes in Central London are of the most help to you. Bus fares are calculated by the distance, as are those of the Underground. You board from the rear, seat yourself either on the main level or upstairs (where you may smoke). Simply state your destination to the conductor when he approaches, pay the requested amount, retaining the ticket you are given, in case you are later asked to produce it. Bus conductors—traditionally Cockney, and either male or female—are now West Indian and East Indian, as well. Like their Underground colleagues, they are the traveler's best friends in London; feel free to ask for their help.

London's *taxis* are especially designed as taxis, with plenty of leg room in front of one, and plenty of head room so that it's easy to step in and out; they are the most civilized such conveyances of any country on the planet. They are metered, but nominal extra charges are made for luggage, and drivers are tipped (see below). They may be hailed as they pass or picked up at taxi-ranks, of which there are many. Taxi-ranks have phones. Two worth knowing are St. George's Square (834-1014) and Sloane Square (730-2664). Hotel doormen are expert at securing taxis, and you need not be a guest at the hotel to ask the doorman's help in this regard; naturally, he will expect a tip for his service.

Self-drive cars are obtainable from a great number of firms. The two American leaders, *Avis* (245-9862) and *Hertz* (837-3898) are both on the scene, but so are many English firms, of which *Godfrey Davis* (834-8484) and *J. Davy* (373-6000) are among the best known.

Private escorted sight-seeing: Several firms specialize in tailor-made touring. One such, *Grosvenor Guide Service* (13a Harriet Walk) is operated by the knowledgeable Mrs. Judy Hoade and a staff of modish, educated ladies, all of them trained and licensed guides. Mrs. Hoade or one of her colleagues will take you where you want to go; they use their own cars and act as guide-drivers. If you like, they'll come up with imaginative suggestions for excursions—shopping in town, inspecting an Inn of Court with one of its members, and lunching with him in that Inn's Great Hall; touring Parliament with an insider, and privately; taking in Royal Ascot, or a polo match at Windsor Great Park. And Grosvenor is excellent at country-house tours or other excursions into the countryside. *Take-a-Guide* (5 Lower Sloane Street) and *Call-a-Tour Ltd.* (55a Sloane Square) are similar organizations.

The big travel agencies run a variety of *sight-seeing tours* by bus, both of London proper, of attractions nearby, and longer excursions as well. These include *American Express* (6 Haymarket), *Evan Evans Tours Ltd.* (41 Tottenham Court), *Frames* (25 Tavistock Place) and *Richards* (17 Woburn Place). These firms, and many others, publish gratis booklets outlining their services in detail. You may book with them directly or through the hall porter of your hotel.

London is eminently walkable by oneself, map in hand. But there are organized *walking tours* of the various sections of town, usually on Sunday afternoons, for an hour and a half or two. Many of the walkers are Londoners interested in getting to know their town better, and the tours often conclude with groups of the hikers getting together over tea, coffee or a beer. It's a nice way to meet people. For information, contact *London Unlimited,* 15 Hollybank Hill, Sittingbourne, Kent; *Love London,* 2 Ashburn Gardens; or *Off-Beat Tours,* 66 St. Michael's Street.

London and environs from the Thames is eye-filling and easily undertaken by means of scheduled river boats. One, the *Father Thames,* is actually a restaurant with luncheon and dinner cruises from Cadogan Pier, Chelsea, to Greenwich. Others depart downstream from Westminster Bridge (at Parliament) to the Tower of London (time: 20 minutes) and Greenwich (50 minutes), with frequent departures, usually every 20 minutes during the day. Upstream, they go from Westminster Bridge, usually every half hour, to Hampton Court, stopping enroute at Putney, Kew and Richmond, with the whole journey taking—nearly—four hours; if you like, go one way by boat and return by train.

The Season Ticket to History is a bargain-priced pass. It will admit you to the several hundred ancient monuments and historic buildings under the care of the British government, including many in and about London, and is a tremendous money-saver for inveterate sight-seers. London attractions include the Banqueting House, Whitehall; Hampton Court, the Tower of London, and Chiswick House. The cost (subject to change) is $5.50, and it may be ordered by mail from BritRail Travel International, 270 Madison Avenue, New York, New York 10016.

CLIMATE

Milder than you may think, and frequently drier than you might think. Every season is good for London. Summer (June through August) averages in the sixties, with seventies as highs in July and August, and the occasional scorcher of a heat wave— say, maybe eighty—which throws the town into a tizzy. (There is no real need for air conditioning, so that when it does get hot one feels it; men do especially as there normally is no occasion for them to have the summer-weight suits that Americans habitually wear during the hot-weather months.) Spring (late April and May) and autumn (late September and October) are generally fiftyish. Winter (November through March) averages in the low forties, although thirties weather is not uncommon in January or February.

Moisture of some sort or other can appear at almost any time, not necessarily with notice; that is why Londoners carry umbrellas as habitually as the rest of us do Kleenex. Raincoats—even in summer, which can be cool—are a convenience, too. This is not to say, though, that "bright periods," as the British weathermen call them, are all that infrequent.

CLOTHES

It started in London, the mod-clothes, long-hair phenomenon, and it continues. London is the most tolerant of world capitals—along with New York—as regards attire. Which is not to say that it is not well-dressed. On the contrary, its designers for both men and women are among the most talented extant. And Londoners are clothes-conscious. Better places, particularly after dark, still prefer gents in jackets and ties rather than turtlenecks, and like to see women correspondingly well got up.

CURRENCY

The pound is divided into 100 pence, written "p." There are ½p, 1p, 2p, 5p, 10p and 50p coins; there are £1, £5, £10 and £20 notes, as in the past. You are still likely to come across coins of the old pounds-shillings-pence currency: a shilling is the equal of 5p, and the coins are of the same size; a florin—the two-shilling coin—equals 10p, and the 50p coin is equal to the old 10-shilling note.

ELECTRIC CURRENT

If you bring a shaver, hair dryer, or iron, you'll need a converter gadget; U.S. department stores sell them. London, like all Britain, is on 220 volts—double the 110 of the U.S.A.

THE TIME

London—and all of the UK—is on European time, six hours ahead of Eastern Standard Time in the United States, but only five hours ahead of Eastern Daylight. Add an additional hour's difference each for Central, Mountain and Western U.S. zones.

TIPPING

Generally, restaurants and cafés do not add a service charge, so tip 15 per cent. Tip bellhops and baggage porters 10p per bag. Tip doormen 5p for getting you a cab, unless they have run blocks in the rain, when you might up that to 10p. Tip hall porters—that's English for concierge—an average of 10p–20p per day, but *only* if they've performed special services for you during your stay. (Handing you your key is not a special service.) Tip taxi drivers 10 to 15 per cent, but not less than 7p or 8p. Barbers and hairdressers get 10 per cent, or more—up to 15 per cent—if they've done a super job and the shop is a fancy one. Barmen in pubs are not tipped for the drinks they serve clients at the bar; tip only for service at tables. Hat-check attendants expect ransom in Britain as at home: 2½p usually does it; never more than 5p; about the same for those leechlike washroom attendants who hand you a towel after you've washed your hands.

LANGUAGE

There is a tremendous fuss sometimes made by Britons and Americans as regards the differences between the English spoken in the two countries. In the two decades-plus that I have been visiting Britain, I have never encountered a bit of difficulty, nor do I know anyone else who has. I am not, therefore, about to give you a "vocabulary" of Britishisms; any American with an even average IQ figures these out as they come his way. And vice versa with our British cousins.

LOCAL LITERATURE

Where do you begin with this category, in London of all cities? There are, to start, guide books and picture albums on London of varying quality. The earlier-mentioned *What's On in London* is on sale each week at newsstands, full of information, albeit typographically difficult to plow through. Of the newspapers, I consider the American-edited *International Herald Tribune* (printed partly in England, partly in France) more useful on the Continent than in London, where it seems to me much more to the point for the English-speaking visitor to read the local press, which has the great advantage of being published in his own language. I regularly read *The Guardian* (formerly the *Manchester Guardian,* but for some time published both in London and Manchester); *The Times* of London (the Personals are no longer much fun, but the letters to the editor can be amusing, and the daily *Court Circular* keeps you abreast of what the Royal Family is up to, day in and day out), and *The Daily Telegraph;* these are all national dailies, with *The Guardian* the most politically liberal, *The Telegraph* the least so (although it has a reporting staff, both foreign and domestic, of high caliber); and *The Times* the best of the lot to acquaint oneself with the ramifications of British eccentricity, as witness this, my all-time favorite *Times* Personal:

IDENTICAL TWINS required to travel as social secretary/P.A. to English lady with large family, large house and big headache. Requirements: one of the girls must be able to type, have organized mind and speak French; the other to receive guests, supervise staff and generally organize house. High salary, an interesting life with much travel for the twins that fill these qualifications. Please write first with photo to . . .

Let me give you an idea of how the progressive *Guardian* and that pillar of the Establishment, *The Times,* chronicle the very same event. The Court Circular page of *The Times* (and *The Telegraph* as well, for that matter) contains tightly packed columns on marriages, engagements, birthdays, memorial services and news of the older universities—all having to do primarily with Establishment families. A "Dinners" column story in *The Times* ran thusly—under the subheading, "Prime Minister"—"The Archbishop of Canterbury and Mrs. Ramsey and Cardinal Heenan, Archbishop of Westminster, were present at a dinner given by the Prime Minister at 10 Downing Street yesterday. The other guests were: Cardinal Conway, the Archbishop of Armagh, the Archbishop of Birmington, the Archbishop of Glasgow," etc., etc., etc. for two long paragraphs of tiny, tiny type. In the same day's *Guardian,* there was this story, under the snappy headline, "Clergy Dine at No. 10": "An unprecedented collection of archbishops, bishops, moderators, abbots and assorted clergy, accompanied, where appropriate, by their wives, passed through the doors of 10 Downing Street last night to have dinner with Mr. Heath. They were drawn from many different denominations—Anglican and Catholic, Baptist and Methodist, Episcopalian and Presbyterian, Church in Wales and United Reformed. Statistical returns compiled from the guest list showed there were two Eminences, five Most Reverends, three Very Reverends, 11 Right Reverends and six ordinary Reverends. The laymen, by contrast, were pitifully represented."

And let me also call to your attention a type of journalism unknown in the American press, the almost verbatim-style reporting of Parliamentary debates, at its most typical in *The Times.* A House or Lords column might open up like this: "Lord Shackleton (Lab) said that before the business began he wished to congratulate Lord Windlesham, the new leader of the House and Lord Privy Seal, on taking up great responsibilities and a job which was not always easy but was very rewarding. He also wished to congratulate Lady Young on her meteoric career in becoming a Parliamentary Under Secretary. On behalf of the Opposition, he also wished to extend best wishes to Lord Sanford and Lord Belstead. In congratulating Lord Windlesham, we note (he said) that he is taking on his post at a difficult time." A rather charming feature of this kind of reportage is the use of parenthetical intelligence on the members' reactions to the speeches. These can range from (Laughter) through (Cheers) and (Further Cheers) to (Renewed Cheers).

Withal, the Court Circular reports remain the most fascinating to a foreign visitor. Americans rarely are treated to such detailed chronicles of the comings and goings of their Commander in Chief and First Lady. Some days are of course lighter than others. The long ones are the most fun. Take June 5, 1973. The Buckingham Palace report is loaded with details. It opens dully enough, with "The Hon. Rupert Hamer (Premier of Victoria) having the honor of being received by The Queen." It continues with more Australiana: "Air Marshal Sir Colin Hannah (Governor of Queensland) had the honor of being received by Her Majesty when The Queen invested him with the Insignia of a Knight Commander of the Most Distinguished Order of St. Michael and St. George." Moreover, we learn that Lady Hannah also had the honor of being received by Her Majesty. And that Mr. J. H. Smith had the honor of being received as well, upon his appointment as Governor of the Gilbert and Ellice Islands. Only later on do we learn that "The Right Hon. Edward Heath, MP [Prime Minister and First Lord of the Treasury] had an audience of Her Majesty this evening." And only after that is it recorded that The Duke of Edinburgh left Heathrow Airport, London, this morning in an aircraft of the Queen's Flight to visit Portugal in connection with the 500th anniversary of the Anglo-Portuguese Alliance. Her Majesty was apparently too busy to get to the airport, for it is chronicled that "By command of The Queen the Baroness Young (Baroness in Waiting) was present at Heathrow Airport, London, this morning upon the departure of the Duke of Edinburgh for Portugal and bade farewell to His Royal Highness on behalf of Her Majesty."

Meanwhile, from down the Mall at Clarence House it is reported that Queen Elizabeth the Queen Mother was represented by the Lord Adam Gordon at the Memorial Service for Lieutenant Colonel the Lord Nugent which was held at the Guards Chapel, Wellington Barracks, and that moreover—and perhaps more important—the Lady Elizabeth Basset had succeeded Ruth, Lady Fermoy as Lady-in-Waiting to Her Majesty.

That same day, from out at Kensington Palace, announcement is made of the fact that The Princess Margaret, Countess of Snowdon, visited the Royal Air Force Police Depot, Debden,

Essex, and that Her Royal Highness, who traveled in an aircraft of The Queen's Flight, was attended by the Lady Anne Tennant.

While from York House at St. James's Palace, it is revealed that the Duke of Kent, president of the Royal National Lifeboat Institution, visited lifeboat stations on Solway Firth, and that His Royal Highness, who traveled in an aircraft of The Queen's Flight, was attended by Lieutenant-Commander Richard Buckley, R.N.

Now who says the Royal Family doesn't earn its keep? Certainly not the readers of *The Times,* neither native nor transatlantic.

The other papers are more easily skippable, although you might enjoy William Hickey's gossipy column in the *Daily Express*—a paper which is published for the masses and can be read through in about eight minutes. I frequently pick up, also, the well-edited *Financial Times,* which has a lot more to it than business and financial news. Of the afternoon papers, I rather like the tightly edited, tabloid-size *Standard.* The Sunday papers, with the exception of *The Sunday Telegraph,* are all separate publications —not the Sunday edition of dailies. *The Telegraph,* along with *The Observer* and *The Sunday Times* (which has the same proprietor as the daily *Times* but is not the same paper), are the top three, with excellent background features; high-caliber criticism of books, plays, music and movies; and innovative typographic design that has not yet been emulated by most American newspapers. All three are eminently readable. There remain the sensational Sunday press; it puts the popular papers among the dailies to shame. Its stars are *The News of the World* (which claims the largest circulation on the planet—well over six million) and *The People,* with a somewhat (but not much) smaller readership. Try them; you may (or may not) be amused. (In my view, *The People* is the more fun of the two.) But contemporary Britain would not be contemporary Britain without them.

British magazines appear to continue to thrive, unlike so many of their American cousins. The political weeklies are excellent, most especially the liberal *New Statesman and Nation* and the conservative *Economist,* with the also-conservative *Spectator* of interest, too. The glossies are beautiful to look upon and many of them make good reading. I have always been partial to the *Illustrated London News,* and although I do not always find myself able to laugh at its cartoons (you must be British for some of these), I enjoy *Punch*. *Queen* is a super slick, and the British editions (locally produced) of *Vogue* and *House and Garden* are worth perusing, while *The Tattler* takes up where the daily Court Circular—and the surrounding announcements in *The Times* and *Telegraph* on the Establishment's comings and goings —leave off. Very worth one's acquaintance, too, is *Private Eye,* a remarkably—and much remarked upon—satirical bi-monthly.

NEGOTIATING THE PUBLIC TELEPHONE

What is important to remember is that you don't insert the money—a 2p coin for local calls in London—until you have dialed your number and hear a rapid *peep-peep* signal. With the advent of the peep-peeps, plunge your 2p coin into the slot, and when your party has answered, you are ready to communicate. (The Button B, which one had to remember to push before being able to speak, is, blessedly, no longer a part of the public telephone apparatus except in remote rural areas.) The busy signal is not all that different from our own, albeit a little more musical and higher-pitched. If you have problems, dial 100 and ask the operator for help; dial the same number if you want to call collect, using the term "reverse charge." Information is 192. It is possible to dial a transatlantic number by yourself, but you are better off letting your hotel operator help you with this type of call or, indeed, for a long-distance call within Britain or to Continental Europe. Calls across the English Channel to the Continent, especially during weekday business hours, can take time and are best made, I find, from the comfort of one's hotel room, with the aid of one's hotel operator. One additional point: The area code of London numbers is 0l; ignore it when dialing a number from within the city.

SOME USEFUL ADDRESSES AND TELEPHONE NUMBERS

The *Thomas Cook money-changing office* at Victoria Station is open daily, including Sunday, from 8:15 A.M. to 10 P.M. You may also change money at the *Buckingham Palace Road Air Terminal* daily including Sunday from 7:30 A.M. to 11 P.M., and note that there are money-changing offices at *Harrods* (Knightsbridge) and *D. H. Evans* (Oxford Street) department stores, not to mention the regular *banks* which are open 9:30 A.M. to 3:30 P.M. Monday through Friday, and one late afternoon a week. If you hold an American Express credit card and need money, present it at an *American Express* office (Haymarket or the Savoy Hotel among others) and upon presentation of your personal check you may obtain up to $450 in traveler's checks and up to $50 in cash. The *Trafalgar Square Post Office* never, ever closes . . . The *Boots Chemists* on Piccadilly Circus never closes, important to remember in case of emergency prescriptions . . . *St. George's Hospital,* the handsome early-nineteenth-century building at Hyde Park Corner, operates a 24-hour emergency service . . . The *London Taxi Lost & Found* is at 15 Renton Street . . . The *All-Purpose Emergency Telephone Number*—for police, fire, and ambulance—is 999. You may dial it from any telephone—and for free; no coin is necessary. Dial 246-8041 for the *London Tourist Board's* daily recorded roundup of visitor attractions; dial 730-0791 for answers to specific tourists questions by the Board; and dial 730-9845 for help from the Board on booking hotels. *London Transport's* phone number—for information on the Underground and buses—is 222-1234, round-the-clock. *The American Embassy* (including Consulate General and Commercial Attaché) is on Grosvenor Square (telephone: 499-9000). *The Canadian High Commission* is at Canada House, Trafalgar Square (telephone: 930-9741). And lastly, the weather: dial 246-8091 for the latest prediction.

BUSINESS HOURS

Regular daily hours are from about 9 A.M. to about 5:30 P.M., Monday through Friday. However, many shops close Saturday at 1 P.M., and some—in London these are mainly in Chelsea and Soho—close Thursday at 1 P.M., instead remaining open until 5:30 P.M. on Saturday. The department stores, bless 'em, remain

open all day Saturday until 5:30 P.M. Additionally, they usually
have one open evening a week—I say evening rather than night
because it's not very late. With Harrods in Knightsbridge, this
traditionally has been Wednesday. Oxford Street department stores
—Selfridges and its neighbors—stay open late on Thursday.

Banks are open Monday through Friday from 9:30 A.M. to
3:30 P.M. and one late afternoon a week.

FURTHER INFORMATION

Before you leave North America, write (or, better yet, visit)
the *British Tourist Authority,* with offices at 680 Fifth Avenue,
New York; John Hancock Center, Chicago; 612 South Flower
Street, Los Angeles; 1712 Commerce Street, Dallas; 151 Bloor
Street West, Toronto; and 602 West Hastings Street, Vancouver.
In New York, BTA's help-yourself racks—a whole room full of
free pamphlets and brochures, arranged by category (transport, hotels, sight-seeing, etc.)—is quite unlike any other government tourist office's system, there being no need to patiently beg an attend-
ant for each folder that you want. BTA's London office is similarly
organized. In London, the British Tourist Authority is at 64 St.
James's Street. The *London Tourist Board's* headquarters are at
4 Grosvenor Gardens, and there are branches in Victoria Station,
and at 8–10 Buckingham Palace Road, this last for student in-
quiries. *London Transport Information Bureaus* are located in
the Piccadilly Circus, Oxford Circus, King's Cross, St. James's
Park, Victoria and Euston Underground stations; they're usually
open from 8:30 A.M. until 9:30 P.M. every day. The earlier-mentioned *British Rail Travel Centre* is at 12 Lower Regent Street.
And when you are wandering around the City and would like some
sight-seeing suggestions and documentation on that area of town,
stop in at the *City of London Information Centre,* St. Paul's
Churchyard.

Index

Acknowledgments

Many friends and colleagues on both sides of the Atlantic have been helpful to me in connection with the preparation of this book. I am especially grateful to James Turbayne, O.B.E., Edmund Antrobus, Andrew Glaze and Mrs. Millicent McCaffrey, of the British Tourist Authority's New York office; Peter ffrench-Hodges, of BTA's headquarters in London; Mrs. Judy Hoade, director of the Grosvenor Guide Service, London; Max Drechsler, my research editor, for considerable help with on-the-spot investigations in London, a city in which he has lived and knows well; senior editor Lawrence Ashmead of Doubleday—ever-supportive and enthusiastic with this book as with the other A to Zs; assistant editor Michele Tempesta, of Doubleday, for much-appreciated day-by-day help and counsel; cartographer Rafael Palacios, for the handsome map of London designed especially for this book; Miss Marie Haller—as enthusiastic a London buff as myself—for her skillful copy editing; and Miss Louise Fisher, for her expert typing of the final manuscript. Whatever errors crop up are mine, as are, of course, the opinions expressed.

R.S.K.